THE GOLF CONNOISSEUR

Also by Robert McCord

The 479 Best Public Golf Courses in the United States, Canada, the Caribbean and Mexico

The Golf Book of Days

The Golf Connoisseur

Robert McCord

LYONS & BURFORD, PUBLISHERS

Printed in the United States of America

Design by LaBreacht Design

10 9 8 7 6 5 4 3 2 1

McCord, Robert R.
    The golf connoisseur / Robert McCord.
       p.   cm..
    ISBN 1-55821-397-X
    1. Golf—Directories. 2. Golf courses—Directories. 3. Golf—Bibliography. 4. Golf—
    Equipment and supplies—Directories. 5. Golf—Collectibles—Catalogs. 6. Golf—
    Museums—Directories.
I. Title.
GV962.M34 1996
796.352'025—dc20   95-46950
                                               CIP

For Helen Reed and Richard S. McCord

Susan McCord Hanley, John, Bob, and Joe

Frank McCord, Barbara, Steve, Sam, Matt, and Kimberly

contents

contents

acknowledgments

There are many people who have helped, directly or indirectly, in assembling this book. Peter Burford, my editor at Lyons & Burford, provided the idea, the inspiration, and the support. Lyons & Burford is one of the few publishers consistently dedicated to publishing golf books, including revivals of quality out-of-print books. I am grateful for the help provided by Karen Bednarski, Nancy Stulack, and others at the United States Golf Association; Marge Dewey at the Ralph Miller Library; and golf clubs including the James River Country Club Museum, the Atlanta Athletic Club, and others. Organizations such as the Golf Collector's Society, the Donald Ross Society, and others have been extremely helpful and should be congratulated on their dedication to the best traditions of the game.

Special thanks to George and Susan Lewis of Golfiana in Mamaroneck, New York, who are ever helpful.

And thanks to my wife Nancy, who is always supportive and is an excellent editor and critic.

—Robert McCord
New York City

The Golf Connoisseur is indeed a pretentious name. But why not? Over the years I have collected a considerable amount of information about golf and have tried to keep up with its dynamic changes. Most notable among these is the growth of golf:

introduction

During the past thirty-five years the number of golfers in the United States alone has increased from five million to over twenty-five million. Needless to say, with this growth has come an avalanche of new courses, equipment, instructional aids, publications, rules changes, tournaments, organizations, and businesses that are mind-boggling in their numbers and complexity.

Golf itself is a simple enough game. A player strikes a ball toward a target and hopes to get there with some degree of proficiency. But the terrain always varies, suggesting that indeed the game can become complex rather quickly. In the old days this golfing effort took place on informal, rude linksland layouts where herds grazed and people strolled. Usually no score was kept, but perhaps one would place a friendly wager on a match play contest for a grog or two.

Now it seems we require manicured golf courses, elegant clubhouses, the latest in high-tech equipment, instructional gurus, and a plethora of instructional aids to outwit the gods of golf. With this I can't help wondering whether the game has become too commercialized, too expensive, and too complex in an unnecessary way. I also wonder if all these machinations in the world of golf have taken some of the fun out of this most elegant and frustrating game.

That having been said, the attempt here is to cull and organize the best of golf's various elements—courses, equipment, books, museums, instruction, organizations, and the like—to provide a road map that might be useful to the golfer who needs a quick reference or an informational compass in golf's kingdom.

In compiling a volume such as this, the author invariably has some blind spots and makes omissions of sources that arguably should be included. Any suggestions or constructive criticism regarding this book are welcome. Please direct them to my attention at the publisher's address. Any mistakes, bad judgment, slices, shanks, or whiffs are, of course, the author's responsibility.

Museums and collections are, in a sense, the contributors to golf's collective memory. There is something about seeing an oil painting of a seventeenth-century royal golfer or viewing an old featherie ball that makes us aware of golf's rich history. An awareness of and appreciation for this history adds enjoyment to the game, especially for one like myself who is not overly good at playing it. In golf, there is always something—the courses, the equipment, the personalities, the literature—that adds another element to the game.

1

golf museums
and collections

Theories abound as to how and where the game of golf originated. Some would have you believe that the Egyptians were the first duffers, and to this day there is a golf course within walking distance of the Sphinx. Others would tell us that the Romans, who played a game called *paganica*, which involved the use of a bent stick and a ball stuffed with wool batted around in the open countryside, were the pioneers of golf. Some historians claim that as the Roman Empire moved west, so did *paganica*; variations of the game appeared on the frozen rivers of Holland and in the countryside of Western Europe and England. The Dutch had a four-hole golf course as early as 1297. The game spread throughout Dutch communities and was depicted in paintings as early as the sixteenth century. During a recent excavation for a subway route in Amsterdam, a beechwood golf ball dating from the late 1500s and fragments of golf clubs were unearthed. These clubs were made of hazelwood and had lead shafts. Leather-covered balls stuffed with cow's hair were also used at the time.

In the aftermath of the Roman Empire, variations of golf were played in France and Belgium (called *choulla* or *choulle*) but golfe, as the locals called it, quickly became the enduring national pastime of the Scots. The Scottish game involved the use of several types of clubs to strike a ball over a set course toward a series of holes in the ground. The early Dutch game often had stakes as the target. Golf became so popular in Scotland that King James II issued an edict to Parliament in 1457 that forbade the playing of golf. The king wanted the locals to concentrate on archery, then critical to the national defense. Golf continued to be played however, especially by King James II, who often combined castle tours of the realm with forays onto the linksland. In 1994, Bob Pringle, proprietor of Old Troon Sporting Antiques in Scotland, claimed to have found a club, circa 1502, made for King James IV, another royal duffer.

By the middle of the eighteenth century, golfing societies had been formed, the most notable having been the Royal and Ancient Golf Club of St. Andrews, which came into existence in 1754, nineteen years after the Royal Burgess Golfing Society of Edinburgh, Scotland—the longest continuously operating golfing society or club in the world. The Society of St. Andrews Golfers were made up of noblemen and lairds, university professors, and professional men. In 1764 the number of holes on the original Old Course at St. Andrews was reduced from 22 to 18, which gradually became the standard-length golf course. The relatively high cost of golf equipment, most notably the leather-covered feather-stuffed featherie ball, which took a craftsman two hours to make, limited the spread of golf.

The Society of St. Andrews Golfers adopted the code of rules laid down by the Honorable Company of Edinburgh Golfers. In 1834 the club applied to King William IV for permission to take the name Royal and Ancient Golf Club and persuaded him to become the first captain of the newly named club. In 1854 the present clubhouse was opened. The Royal and Ancient was one of the select clubs on the committee to start the British Open, which first officially took place on the 12-hole Prestwick Course, where three rounds were played in October of 1860.

The first Open was not open to amateurs, but they were admitted to the second event and have played ever since.

In 1897 the Royal and Ancient agreed to become the governing authority on the rules of golf. The United States Golf Association (USGA) was established in 1894 by members of five clubs: the Newport Golf Club (Newport, Rhode Island), the St. Andrews Golf Club (Yonkers, New York), the Country Club (Brookline, Massachusetts), the Chicago Club (Chicago, Illinois), and the National Golf Links (Southampton, Long Island, New York). The USGA sponsored the U.S. Open and U.S. Amateur, both first played at the Newport Golf Club in October of 1895. In May 1951, twelve representatives from the governing bodies of golf in Great Britain, Australia, Canada, and the United States met in London to develop a code of rules golf that is now used uniformly throughout the world. Quadrennial Rules Conferences are held to update the rules.

The United States Golf Association, based in Far Hills, New Jersey, now represents more than eight thousand member clubs and courses. The primary responsibilities of the organization are to oversee rules and competitions and to provide general services such as those afforded by its Green Section, which, since 1920, has assisted in research and development in raising the maintenance and playing standards of golf courses. The USGA conducts thirteen national championships and, in cooperation with the Royal and Ancient, conducts the International Match for the Walker Cup (established in 1922), a biennial competition between teams of male amateur golfers, the United States on one side and Great Britain and Ireland on the other. Since 1932, the USGA, with the British Ladies Golf Union, has conducted the International Match for the Curtis Cup, played between teams of female amateur players from the United States and from Great Britain and Ireland. The USGA is also active within the World Amateur Golf Council, which has conducted the World Amateur Team Championship since 1958 and the Women's World Amateur Team Championship since 1964.

The United States Golf Association maintains a museum and library at Golf House, a brick mansion adjacent its headquarters in Far Hills, New Jersey. Golf House is the name of a building where early members of the Society of St. Andrews Golfers first met before they relocated to at the Union Parlour and, still later (currently), to the clubhouse at St. Andrews. The USGA library contains more than eight thousand golf volumes, and the museum offers a variety of informative exhibits including permanent displays tracing the history of golf, collections of Bobby Jones memorabilia, and more. The Royal and Ancient is the governing body of golf throughout the world, with the exception of the United States and Mexico. Below is a short list of museums that preserve an interesting assortment of golf literature, equipment, and other related treasures. Contact the museums directly for hours, directions, and special exhibits.

MUSEUMS AND LIBRARIES

Eastern United States

American Golf Classics
12842 Jefferson Avenue
Newport News, VA 23602
(703) 874-7271

The American Golf Hall of Fame
Foxburg Country Club
Box 305
Harvey Road
Foxburg, PA 16036
(412) 659-3196

James River Country Club Museum
1500 Country Club Road
Newport News, VA 23606
(804) 596-4772

Ladies Professional Golf Association
2570 W. International
   Speedway Boulevard
Suite B
Daytona Beach, FL 32114-
   1118
(904) 254-8800

The Ouimet Room
Massachusetts Golf
   Association
190 Park Road
Weston, MA
(617) 891-6400

The PGA World Golf Hall of Fame
c/o PGA of America
P.O. Box 109601
Palm Beach Gardens, FL
   33418
(407) 624-8400

The United States Golf Association Museum and Library
P.O. Box 708
Route 512
Far Hills, NJ 07931
(908) 234-2300

Midwestern United States

Chicago District Golf Association
619 Enterprise
Suite 101
Oak Brook, IL 60521
(708) 954-2180

Rev. Edmund P. Joyce Sports Research Collection
102 Hesburgh Library
Notre Dame, IN 46556
(219) 631-5252

Western Golf Association
1 Briar Road
Golf, Il 60029
(312) 724-4600

Western United States

Ralph W. Miller Golf Museum and Library
One Industry Hills
    Parkway
City of Industry, CA 91744
(818) 854-2354

Northern California Golf Association
Box 1157
Pebble Beach, CA 93953
(408) 625-4653

Jude E. Poynter Golf Museum
College of the Desert
43-500 Monterey Avenue
Palm Desert, CA 92260
(619) 341-2491

Canada

The British Columbia Golf House Society
2545 Blanca Street
Vancouver,
British Columbia, Canada
(604) 222-4653

Canadian Golf Museum and Historical Institute
Kingsway Park Golf and
Country Club
1461 Mountain Road
R. R. #2, Aylmer East
Quebec
J9H 5E1 Canada
(819) 827-0030

Royal Canadian Golf Association
Glen Abbey Golf Club
R. R. #2, Golf House
Oakville, Ontario
Canada L6J 4Z3
(416) 844-1800

International

The British Golf Museum
St. Andrews, Fife
Scotland
(44) 0334 73423

The Heritage of Golf
West Links Road
Gullane, East Lothian,
Scotland
(44) 08757 277

Japan Golf Association Museum
Palace Building
6th Floor
Tokyo, Japan

Royal North Devon Golf Club Museum at Westward Ho!
Westward Ho!, Devon
England
(44) 02372 3824

EXHIBITS AT GOLF CLUBS

Atlanta Athletic Club
Robert Trent Jones, Jr.
    Room
Athletic Club Drive
Duluth, GA 30136
(404) 448-2166

Baltusrol Golf Club
Shunpike Road
Springfield, NJ 07081
(201) 376-5160

Broadmoor Golf Club
Lake Avenue and Lake
    Circle
Colorado Springs, CO
    80901
(719) 577-5775

Colonial Country Club
3735 Country Club
    Circle
Fort Worth, TX 76109
(817) 927-4200

The Greenbrier
Route 60
White Sulphur Springs,
    WV 24986
(304) 536-1110
(800) 624-6070

The Homestead
U.S. 220
Hot Springs, VA 24445
(703) 839-5500
(800) 336-5771
    (outside VA)

**Los Angeles
Country Club**
10101 Wilshire
    Boulevard
Los Angeles, CA 90024
(213) 276-6104

Merion Golf Club
450 Ardmore Avenue
Ardmore, PA 19003
(610) 642-5600.

**National Golf Links
    of America**
Sedonic Inlet Road
Southampton, NY 11968
(516) 283-0410

Oak Hill Country Club
Box 10397
Rochester, NY 14610
(716) 586-1660

Oakmont Country Club
1233 Hulton Road
Oakmont, PA 15139
(412) 828-8000

Old Marsh Golf Club
7500 Old Marsh Road
Palm Beach Gardens, FL
    33418
(407) 626-7400

**Pinehurst Resort and
Country Club**
Carolina/Vista
P.O. Box 4000
Pinehurst, NC 28374
(919) 295-6811
(800) 927-4653 (outside
    NC)

Pine Valley Golf Club
East Atlantic Avenue
Pine Valley, NJ 08021
(609) 783-3000

Winged Foot Golf Club
Fennimore Road
Mamaroneck, NY 10543
(914) 698-8406

While golf is the ultimate test of individual patience and skill, it is also a social game. Inevitably associations were developed to organize, regulate, and promote the sport. One of the longest continuously operating golfing societies or clubs is the Royal Burgess Golfing Society of Edinburgh, Scotland, which was established as the Edinburgh Golf Society in 1735. The Honorable Company of Edinburgh Golfers was established nine years later and the Royal and Ancient, arbiter of golf rules along with the United States Golf Association, in 1754. The first formal rules of golf, delineated by The Honorable Company of Edinburgh Golfers in 1744 were titled "Articles and Laws Playing at Golf." Until 1875 the number of written rules increased by only seven.

Early competitions were usually match play and held on courses with varying numbers of holes, although St. Andrews set the standard when the Old Course was remodeled to become an 18-hole course (it had been 22 holes) in 1764. Stroke play was introduced at St. Andrews in 1759. Individual clubs and societies often had their own interpretations of the rules, and it was not until 1897 that the Royal and Ancient was given the responsibility for framing and interpreting the rules. Rules interpretations were becoming more numerous and more

2

golf associations

complicated as a result of the increased popularity of golf; the development of new equipment (the featherie was superceded by the gutta percha in the 1840s, and the Haskell ball would render the gutty obsolete by the turn of the century); raging debates over tactics such as the stymie; the development of parkland and other types of inland courses; and other changes in the game.

The game of golf spread to North America in the colonial era, and the Montreal Golf Club, later deigned Royal, established in 1873, became the first club there. St. Andrews, established in Yonkers, New York, in 1888, is credited with being the first continously operating golf club in the United States, although golf was played in the New World since the seventeenth century. The United States Golf Association was formed in 1894, primarily to organize events, preside over national championships, and arbitrate rules. As time went on, a need arose for international coordination and standardization of rules and events. The Royal and Ancient and the United States Golf Association stepped in to serve as legislators and regulators of the game in coordination with golf associations around the world.

Allan Robertson, born in St. Andrews, Fife, Scotland, in 1815 is considered one of the best early professional golfers. Before the first British Open was held at Prestwick (three rounds of 12 holes) in 1860, Robertson would team with Old Tom Morris, his assistant, to compete against other golf professionals such as the Dunn brothers of the Musselburgh club. The Professional Golf Association was formed in England in 1918, the Canadian Professional Golfers Association in 1911, and the PGA of America in 1916. The first Canadian Open was held in 1904 at Royal Montreal, the first PGA Championship was held at the Siwanoy Country Club in Bronxville in 1916, and the first U.S. Open was held at the Newport Golf Club in 1895. The inaugural British Amateur was held in 1885 at Hoylake, the Canadian Amateur at Ottawa in 1895, and the U.S. Amateur at Newport in 1895. In that era of gentlemen golfers, the amateur contests were more prestigious than the professional events.

Mary Queen of Scots, the most notable early woman golfer, brought cadets (called caddies by the Scots) over from France in the sixteenth century. By the 1860s British women were establishing their own clubs. The St. Andrews Ladies' Golf Club was formed in 1867, and by 1893 representatives of ten ladies' golf clubs formed the Ladies Golf Union and conducted the British Ladies Amateur

Championship at Royal Lytham and St. Anne's that same year. Lady Margaret Scott, the dominant player of the day, won the first three championships before retiring to become Lady Margaret Hamilton-Russell. The first Canadian national women's championship, the Canadian Ladies Amateur was held at Royal Montreal and won by Ms. L. Young in 1901. Mrs. C. S. Brown won the first U.S. Women's Amateur held at the Meadow Brook Club in Hempstead, New York, in 1895. The first dominant American female golfer was Beatrix Hoyt who won the next three championships before she retired from tournament golf at age 20. The first U.S. Women's Open was not played until 1946, when professional golf was becoming a viable career for American women. Patty Berg, who began her professional career in 1940 after posting an outstanding amateur record, won that event at the Spokane Country Club in Washington. The Ladies Professional Golf Association of America was formed in 1949, and the LPGA Tour began in 1950.

Golf is now an international game with golf associations and tournaments worldwide. It is also more vertically organized, with cradle-to-grave programs and tournaments such as the Girls' Junior Championship (established in 1949) and the Junior Amateur Championship (1948) through the Senior Women's Amateur Championships (1962) and the Senior Amateur Championship (1955), all USGA-organized events. Premiere international competitions such as the International Match for the Walker Cup (1922), the International Match for the Ryder Cup (1927), the International Match for the Curtis Cup (1932), and others reinforce golf's impact around the world.

In the old days, the club professional was often the greenkeeper, course designer or remodeler, teacher, club maker, ball maker, match competitor, and general jack-of-all-trades. In the Old World, he was less educated and of lower social standing than the gentry who usually ran the club. This tradition continued into the colonies as golf clubs and golf associations often became an old-boy's network that reinforced familial, social, ethnic, religious, educational, and economic ties. These barriers to entry have gradually broken down as golf has become more commonly played across all levels of society. At the same time, organizations and associations reflecting the increased complexity of the game off the course have been formed. These include groups such as the Golf Collector's Society, the Association of Golf Merchandisers, the Golf Writers Association of America, the National Association of Left-handed Golfers, the Tournament Sponsors Association, the American Society of Golf Course Architects, and many others.

Below is a selected list of golf associations. A more complete list can be obtained from the National Golf Foundation, 1150 South U.S. Highway One, Suite 405, Jupiter, FL 33477 (800) 733-6006, (407) 744-6006.

GOLF ASSOCIATIONS AND RELATED ORGANIZATIONS

United States

Amateur Athletic Foundation
2141 West Adams
   Boulevard
Los Angeles, CA 90018
(213) 730-9696

American Association of Real Golfers
1522 N.W. 26th Place
Cape Coral, FL 33909
(813) 283-3393
Fax: (813) 772-2149

American Golf Sponsors, Inc.
4 Sawgrass Village
Suite 140 F
Ponte Vedra Beach, FL
   32082
(904) 285-4222
Fax: (904) 285-9713

American Junior Golf Association, Inc.
2415 Steeplechase Lane
Roswell, GA 30076
(404) 998-4653
Fax: (404) 992-9763

American Modified Golf Association
P.O. Box 5287
Albany, GA 31706
(912) 883-5017
(800) 344-0220
Fax: (912) 883-4825

American Society of Golf Course Architects
221 N. LaSalle Street
Chicago, IL 60601
(312) 372-7090
Fax: (312) 372-6160

American Society of Irrigation Consultants
P.O. Box 426
Byron, CA 94514-0426
(510) 516-1124
Fax: (510) 516-1301

Association of Disabled American Golfers
7700 E. Arapahoe Road
Suite 350
Englewood, CO 80112
(303) 220-0921

Association of Golf Merchandisers
16743 E. Palisades
Suite 202
Fountain Hills, AZ 85268
(602) 837-0708
Fax: (602) 837-6658

Business and Charity Golf Link
4450 California Avenue
Suite K-362
Bakersfield, CA 93309
(805) 322-5601

Club Managers Association of America
1733 King Street
Alexandria, VA
   22314-2702
(703) 739-9500
Fax: (703) 739-0124

USGA RECORDS

Among the most significant tournaments the USGA sponsors are the U.S. Open, U.S. Amateur, U.S. Women's Open, and U.S. Women's Amateur .

The U.S. Open title was first decided from a field of eleven players in 1895. The event had over 6,200 entrants in 1992.

- Jack Nicklaus and Lee Janzen hold the record for low winning score, 272.
- Willie Smith holds the record for largest winning margin, eleven strokes, at the Baltimore Country Club in 1899.
- The shortest course played on was Shinnecock Hills, which measured 4,423 yards in 1896.
- The golfers to win the most Opens are Willie Anderson (1901, '03, '04, '05), Robert T. Jones, Jr. (1923, '26, '29, '30), Ben Hogan (1948, '50, '51, '53), and Jack Nicklaus (1962, 67, '72, '80).
- The last amateur to win the U.S. Open was Johnny Goodman, who won in 1933.

The U.S. Amateur, which was first played in 1895, was also won by Goodman in 1933. Only thirty-two players entered the first Amateur, and more than 5,600 signed up in 1993.

- Bobby Jones was the youngest player to compete in the Amateur when he was fourteen years and five months old in 1916.
- Edrick "Tiger" Woods became the youngest winner of this event when he defeated Trip Kuehne at the Stadium Course at TPC Sawgrass in 1994. Woods was eighteen years and seven months old at the time.
- Bobby Jones still holds the record for most tournaments won. He collected five championships in 1924, '25, '27, '28, and '30.

The U.S. Women's Open was first played in 1946. That event was match play, but it changed to medal play the following year.

- Mickey Wright (1958, '59, '61, '64) and Betsy Rawls (1951, '53, '57, '60) have each won four Opens to hold the record.
- French golfer Catherine Lacoste is the only amateur and the youngest golfer to win the Open. She won the event at age twenty-two at the Virginia Hot Springs Cascades Course in 1967.

The U.S. Women's Amateur was first played in 1895 at the Meadow Brook Club in Hempstead, New York, and was won by Mrs. C. S. Brown with an 18-hole score of 132. The Women's Amateur became a match-play event in 1896, and Beatrix Hoyt won three in a row. Ms. Hoyt was sixteen years and three months old when she won her first title. Other sixteen-year-old champions include Laura Baugh (1971), the youngest to win this event; Vicki Goetze (1989) and Michiko Hattori (1985). Only thirteen golfers entered the first U.S. Women's Amateur; a total of 451 entered in 1994.

- Glenna Collett Vare holds the record with six championships (1922, '25, '28, '29, '30, '35). JoAnne Gunderson Carner won five before turning professional (1957, '60, '62, '66, '68).

BILL WRIGHT, then a senior at Western Washington College near Seattle, became the first African-American to win a USGA title when he won the 1959 U.S. Public Links Championship at the age of twenty-three. There were a total of 2,435 entries and 150 qualifiers for the match-play event, which, was held at the Wellshire Golf Course, a 6,617-yard, par-71 layout in Denver. Wright played with two woods, nine irons, and a putter as he won six matches, including a 3 and 2 win over Frank W. Campbell of Jacksonville, Flordia, in the 36-hole final. The first 4 rounds included 18-hole matches, and the semifinal and final rounds were 36-hole contests.

Executive Women's Golf League
1401 Forum Way
Suite 100
West Palm Beach, FL
   33401
(407) 471-1477
Fax: (407) 684-6890

Futures Golf Tour
2003 U.S. 27 South
Sebring, FL 33870-4929
(813) 385-3320

Golf Collectors Society
P.O. Box 20546
Dayton, OH 45420
(513) 256-2474

Golf Course Builders Association of America
920 Airport Road,
Suite 210
Chapel Hill, NC 27514
(919) 942-8922
Fax: (919) 942-6955

Golf Course Superintendents Association of America
1421 Research Park Drive
Lawrence, KS
   66049-3859
(913) 841-2240
(800) 472-7878
Fax: (913) 832-4466

The Golf Intructors and Coaches Association
JFK Government Center
   Station
P.O. Box 8279
Boston, MA 02114-8279
(508) 535-5205
Fax: (508) 535-5205

Golf Manufacturers and Distributors Association
P.O. Box 37324
Cincinnati, OH 45222

Golf Range and Recreation Association of America
211 West 92nd Street
Suite 58
New York, NY 10025
(212) 995-7619
Fax: (212) 677-1562

Golf Writers Association of America
P.O. Box 328054
Farmington Hills, MI
   48332
(313) 442-1481

Indoor Golf Association of America
2665 Ariane Drive
Suite 208
San Diego, CA
92117-3472
(619) 273-0373
Fax: (619) 273-1132

International Association of Golf Administrators
3740 Cahuenga
    Boulevard
North Hollywood, CA
    91609
(818) 980-3630
Fax: (818) 980-1808

International Golf Association
3 East 54th Street
12th Floor
New York, NY 10022
(212) 223-4693

Junior Golf Alliance
3134 Chelmsford Road
Tallahassee, FL 32308
(904) 893-2991
Fax: (904) 893-7209

Ladies Professional Golf Association
2570 W. International
    Speedway Boulevard
Suite B
Daytona Beach, FL 32114
(904) 254-8800
Fax: (904) 254-4755

Miniature Golf Association of America
P.O. Box 32353
Jacksonville, FL 32337
(904) 781-4653
Fax: (904) 260-4549

Minority Golf Association of America
9 Columbia Avenue
P.O. Box 1081
Westhampton, NY 11977
(516) 653-6008
Fax: (516) 288-8255

National Amputee Golf Association
11 Walnut Hill Road
P.O. Box 1228
Amherst, NH
03031-1228
(603) 673-1135
(800) 633-6242
Fax: (603) 672-7140

National Association of Intercollegiate Athletics (NAIA)
1221 Baltimore Avenue
Kansas City, MO 64105
(913) 993-1903

National Association of Left-handed Golfers
P.O. Box 801223
Houston, TX 77280
(713) 464-8683

National Club Association
3050 K Street N.W.
Suite 330
Washington, DC 20007
(202) 625-2080
Fax: (202) 625-9044

National Collegiate Athletic Association (NCAA)
6201 College Boulevard
Overland Park, KS 66211
(913) 339-1906
Fax: (913) 339-1950

National Golf Car Manufacturers Association
2 Ravinia Drive
Suite 1150
Atlanta, GA 30346
(404) 394-7200
Fax: (404) 395-7698

National Golf Course Owners Association
1461 Center Street Ext.
Suite B-1
Mt. Pleasant, SC 29464
(803) 881-99567
(800) 933-4262
Fax: (803) 881-9958

National Golf Foundation
1150 South U.S.
    Highway One
Jupiter, FL 33477
(407) 744-6006
Fax: (407) 744-6107

National Golf Reporters Association Scorecard
P.O. Box 951422
Lake Mary, FL
32795-1422
(407) 774-1464
Fax: (407) 788-8909

National Golf Salesman's Association
P.O. Box 6134
Scottsdale, AZ 85261
(602) 860-6348
Fax: (602) 860-6919

National Junior College Athletic Association
P.O. Box 7305
Colorado Springs, CO
80933
(719) 590-9788
Fax: (719) 590-7324

PGA of America
100 Avenue of the
Champions
Palm Beach Gardens, FL
33418
(407) 624-8400
Fax: (407) 624-7865

PGA Tour
112 TPC Boulevard
Sawgrass
Ponte Vedra, FL 32082
(904) 285-3700
Fax: (904) 285-2460

Professional Clubmakers Society
70 Persimmon Ridge Drive
Louisville, KY 40245
(502) 241-2816

Professional Club Repairman's Association
2053 Harvard Avenue
Dunedin, FL 34698
(813) 733-4348

Professional Putters Association
P.O. Box 35237
Fayetteville, NC
28303-5237
(910) 485-7131
Fax: (910) 485-1122

Senior Masters Golf Association
13042 Betsworth Road
Valley Center, CA 92082
(619) 749-4311

GOLF NUT SOCIETY OF AMERICA is, not surprisingly, an organization of golf fanatics. A lifetime membership, which costs only $25.00, will provide you with buying-club golf-merchandise discounts, golf travel discounts, golf nut getaways to places like Scotland for reduced rates, and access to "The Golf Nut Network" of golf nuts. The organization selects a "Golf Nut of the Year" for devotedness beyond the call of duty. And a national Golf Nut championship is annually held at a fancy resort. Other Golf Nut perks, such as logoed merchandise, bag tags, a membership certificate and more, are available once you join.

Contact: Golf Nut Society of America, P.O. Box 1226, Carefree, AZ 85377.

Society of Golf Appraisers
201 South Orange Avenue
Suite 1400
Orlando, FL 32801
(407) 843-4020
Fax: (407) 839-3171

Sporting Goods Manufacturers Association
200 Castlewood Drive
North Palm Beach, FL 33408-5696
(407) 842-4100
Fax: (407) 863-8984

Statistical Golf Association—Stroke Trac
4950 MacArthur Boulevard, 5th Floor
Newport Beach, CA 92660
(714) 752-7828
Fax: (714) 752-5960

Tournament Sponsors Association
604 Country Club Drive
Stockbridge, GA 30281
(404) 474-0258
Fax: (404) 474-5637

USA Junior Golf Association
905 E. Camp McDonald Road
Prospect Heights, IL 60070
(708) 394-5014

United States Golf Association
P.O. Box 708
Far Hills, NJ 07931-0708
(908) 234-2300
Fax: (908) 234-9687

United States Golf Teachers Association
P.O. Box 3325
Fort Pierce, FL 34948
(407) 464-3272
(800) 365-6727
Fax: (800) 365-6727

United States Putting Association
27-A Big Spring Road
Box 430
Clear Spring, MD 21722
(301) 791-9332

Canada

Alberta Golf Association
104-4116th 64th Avenue S.E.
Calgary, Alberta T2C 2B3
Canada
(403) 236-4616

British Columbia Golf Association
6450 Roberts Street
Suite 185
Sperling Plaza 2
Burnaby, British Columbia V5G 4E1
Canada
(604) 294-1818
Fax: (604) 294-1819

Canadian Golf Foundation
Golf House
1333 Dorval Drive
Oakville, Ontario L6J 4Z3
Canada
(416) 849-9700
(800) 434-6434
Fax: (416) 845-7040

**Canadian Golf
Superintendents
Association**
5580 Explorer Drive
No. 509
Mississauga, Ontario
L4W 4YI
Canada
(905) 602-8873
(800) 387-1056
Fax: (905) 602-1958

**Canadian Ladies Golf
Association**
1600 James Naismith
Gloucester, Ontario
K1B 5N4
Canada
(613) 748-5642

**Canadian Professional
Golfers Association**
R.R. No. 1
13450 Dublin Lane
Acton, Ontario L7J 2W7
Canada
(519) 853-5450
Fax: (519) 853-5449

**Manitoba Golf
Association**
200 Main Street
Winnipeg, Manitoba
R3C 4M2
Canada
(204) 985-4057
Fax: (204) 985-4026

**New Brunswick
Golf Association**
65 Brunswick Street
Fredericton,
New Brunswick
E3B 1G5
Canada
(506) 459-5675

**Nova Scotia Golf
Association**
14 Limardo Drive
Dartmouth, Nova Scotia
B3A 3X4
Canada
(902) 465-7306

**Ontario Ladies Golf
Association**
1220 Sheppard Avenue
East
Willowdale, Ontario
L3Y 4W1
Canada
(416) 495-4130

**Prince Edward Island
Golf**
P.O. Box 51
Charlottetown
Prince Edward Island
CIA 7K2
Canada
(902) 368-1161

**Quebec Golf
Association**
P.O. Box 399
Pierrefonds, Quebec
H9H 4L1
(514) 620-6565
Fax: (514) 620-3413

**Royal Canadian
Golf Association**
R.R. 2
Oakville, Ontario
L6J 4Z3
Canada
(416) 844-1800

**Saskatchewan Golf
Association**
510 Cynthia Street
Suskatoon, Saskatchewan
S7L 7K7
Canada
(306) 975-0834
Fax: (306) 242-8007

*Mexico, Central
America, and
South America*

**ARGENTINA
Asociación Argentina
de Golf**
Corrientes 538-
Piso 11 y 12
Buenos Aires 1043
Argentina
(54) 1-325 7498/7499
Fax: (54) 1-325 8660/8661

BOLIVIA
**Federación Boliviana
de Golf**
Casilla de Correo 6130
La Paz
Bolivia

BRAZIL
**Confederação
Braseleira de Golf**
Rua 7de Abril
282-s/83
01044 São Paolo
Brazil

CHILE
**Federación Chilena
de Golf**
Vicuña Mackenna 40
 Casilla
Santiago 13307
Chile

COLOMBIA
**Federación Colombia de
Golf**
Carrera 7a, No. 72-64 Of.
 Int. 26
Apatado Areo 90985
Bogotá D.E.
Colombia

COSTA RICA
**Costa Rica Golf
Association**
c/o ANAGOLF
P.O. Box 2031-1000
San José
Costa Rica

ECUADOR
**Federación Ecuatoria
de Golf**
Baquerizo Moreno 1120
P.O. Box 521
Guayaquil
Ecuador

EL SALVADOR
**Asociación
Salvadoreña de Golf**
Apartado Postal 631
San Salvador
El Salvador

GUATEMALA
**Federación
Guatemalteca de Golf**
3a Avenida Finca El Zapote
Zona 2
Guatemala

GUYANA
Guyana Golf Union
c/o Demerara Bauxite Co
 Ltd.
Mackenzie
Guyana

HONDURAS
**Asociación Hondureña
de Golf**
Apartado Postal No.
 68-C
Tegucigalpa, D.C.
Honduras

MEXICO
**Asociación De Golf Valle
de Mexico**
Colegio No. 793
Ped Regal de San Angel
Mexico City 01900
(52) 568-3984

PANAMA
**Panama Golf
Association**
Panama 5
Panama

PARAGUAY
**Asociación Paraguaya de
Golf**
Casilla de Correo 1795
Asunción
Paraguay

**South American Golf
Association**
Hotel del Yacht & Golf
P.O. Box 1795
Paraguay
(595) 2 36 117

VENEZUELA
**Federacion Venezolana
de Golf**
Unidad Comercial "La
 Florida"
Local 5, Avenida Avila
La Florida, Caracas
Venezuela

Bahamas, Bermuda, and Caribbean

BAHAMAS
Bahamas Golf Federation
P.O. Box N-4568
Nassau
Bahamas

BERMUDA
Bermuda Golf Association
Box HM
433, Hamilton HMBX
Bermuda
(809) 238-1367

DOMINICAN REPUBLIC
Dominica Golf Association
P.O. Box 641
Santo Domingo
Dominican Republic
(809) 689-7737

EL SALVADOR
Asociación Salvadoreña de Golf
Apartado Postal 631
San Salvador
El Salvador

JAMAICA
Jamaica Golf Association
P.O. Box 743
Kingston 8
Jamaica
(809) 925-2325

PUERTO RICO
Puerto Rico Golf Association
GPO 3862
San Juan
Puerto Rico
(809) 781-2070

TRINIDAD
Trinidad and Tobago Golf Association
7 A Warner Street
Newton Port of Spain
Trinidad

Europe

AUSTRIA
Osterreichischer Golf Verband
Prinz-Eugen Strasse 12
Vienna A-1040
Austria
(43)1-222-5053245
Fax: (43)1-222-5054962

CZECH REPUBLIC
Czechoslovakian Golf Federation
Na Porici 12
CS-11530 Praha 1
Czech Republic
(42)2-22-52-13874

DENMARK
Danish Golf Union
Golfsvinget 12
DK-2625 Vallenbaek,
Denmark
(45)1-42-640666
Fax: (45)1-43-629193

ENGLAND
Amateur Golf Championship
Royal and Ancient
   Golf Club
St. Andrews, Fife
Scotland
(44) 0334-72112
Fax: (44) 0334-77580

Association of Public Golf Courses
35 Sinclarr Grove
Golders Green
London NW11 9JH
England
(44) 081-458 5433

British Association of Golf Course Architects
5 Oxford Street
Woodstock Oxford
GX7 ITQ
England
(44) 0993-811 976

British Association of Golf Course Constructors
Tellford Farm,
Willingale, Ongar
Essex CM5 OQE
England
(44) 0277-896229
Fax: (44) 0245-491620

British and International Greenkeepers' Association
Aldwark Manor, Aldwark,
Aline
York Y06 2NF
England
(44) 03473-5812
Fax: (44) 03473-8864

English Golf Union
1-3 Upper King Street
Leicester, LE1 6XF
England
(44) 53-355 3042

English Ladies' Golf Association
Edgbaston Golf Club
Church Road
Birmingham, B15 3TB
England
(44) 21-456 2088

The Golf Foundation (Junior Golf for Great Britain and Ireland)
Foundation House
Hanbury Manor
Ware, Herts
SG12 OUH
England
(44) 920-484 044
Fax: (44) 920-484 055

PGA Of England
Apollo House,
The Belfry
Sutton Coldfield
West Midlands,
    B76 9PT
England
(44) 0675-470333
Fax: (44) 0675-470674

Professional Golfers Association
P.O. Box 1314
Crows Nest, NSW 2065
England
(44) 02-4398111
Fax: (44) 02-4397888

Sports Turf Research Institute
Bingley West
Yorkshire BD16 IAU
England
(44) 0274-566131
Fax: (44) 0274-561891

FINLAND
Finnish Golf Union
Radiokatu, 12 SF-00240
Helsinki 145
Finland
(358) 0-1582244
Fax: (358) 0-147145

FRANCE
Fédération Française de Golf
69 Avenue Victor-Hugo
Cedex 16
75783 Paris
France
(33) 45-02-13-55
Fax: (33) 45-00-30-68

GERMANY
Deutschland Golf Verband
Pastfach 2106
Wiesbaden 65011
Germany

GREECE
Hellenic Golf Federation
P.O. Box 70003
GR-166 10 Glyfada
Athens
Greece
(30) 18-941933
Fax: (30) 14-116426

HUNGARY
Hungarian Golf Federation
Magyar Golf Szovseg
c/o Rodata RT
Budapest 1028
Hungary
(36) 11-766722

ICELAND
Golfsamband Islands
P.O. Box 1076
IS-101 Reykjavik
Iceland
(354) 1-68-66-86
Fax: (354) 1-29-52-0

IRELAND
Golfing Union of Ireland
Glencar House
81 Eglington Road
Donnybrook, Dublin 4
Ireland
(353) 1-2694111
Fax: (353) 1-2695368

Irish Ladies' Golf Union
1 Clonskeagy Square
Clonskeagh Road
Dublin 14
Ireland
(353) 1-2696244

ITALY
Federazione Italian Golf
Via Flaminia 388
00196 Roma
Italy
(39) 6-394641
Fax: (39) 6-3220250

LUXEMBOURG
Golf Club Grand Ducal
1, Route de Trève
L-2633 Senningerberg
Grand Duché du
   Luxembourg
Luxembourg
(352) 3-4090

THE NETHERLANDS
Netherlands Golf Federation
P.O. Box 221
3454 2L De Meern
The Netherlands
(31) 3406-21888
Fax: (31) 3406-21177

NORWAY
Norwegian Golf Association
Hauger Skolevei
1351 Rud Oslo
Norway
(47) 25-18800
Fax: (47) 21-32989

PORTUGAL
Federação Portuguesa de Golfë
Rua Almeida Brando, 39
P-1200 Lisboa
Portugal
(351) 1-666126
Fax: (351) 1-666162

SCOTLAND
Scottish Golf Union
The Cottage
181A Whitehouse Road
Barnton
Edinburgh EH4 6BY
Scotland
(44) 31-339-1169
Fax: (44) 31-339-1169

Scottish Golfer's Alliance
5 Deveron Avenue
Gifinock
Glasgow G48 6NH
Scotland

Scottish Ladies' Golfing Association
Room 1010–Terminal
   Building
Prestwick Airport
Prestwick, Ayrshire
   KA9 2PL
Scotland
(44) 292-79582

SLOVENIA
Golf Association of
Slovenia
c/o Golf Club Bled
C. Svbode 13
64260 Bled
Slovenia
(386) 4-78282

SPAIN
Real Federación
Espãnola de Golf
Capitán Haya, 9-50 Sur
E-28020
Spain
(34) 1-5552757
Fax: (34) 1-5563290

SWEDEN
Svenska Golfforbundet
Box 84 (Kevingestrand 20)
S-182 11 Danderyd
Sweden

SWITZERLAND
Association Suisse de
Golf
En Ballegue—
    Case Postale
1066 Epalinges
Switzerland
(41) 21-7843531
Fax: (41) 21-7843536

WALES
Welsh Golfing Union
Powys House
Cwmbran, Gwent
    NP44 1PB
Wales
(44) 633-870261
Fax: (44) 633-871837

Welsh Ladies' Golf
Union
Ysgoldy Gynt,
    Llanhennock
Newport, Gwent
    NP44 1PB
Wales
(44) 633-420642

Africa and the Middle East

BOTSWANA
Botswana Golf Union
P.O. Box 1033
Galoorone
Botswana

CYPRUS
Cyprus Golf Union
c/o JSGC Dhekelia
    BPPO 58
Cyprus

EGYPT
The Egyptian Golf
Federation
Gezira Sporting Club
Gezira, Cairo
Egypt
(20) 2-80-6000

GHANA
Ghana Golf Union
P.O. Box 8
Achimola
Ghana

ISRAEL
Israel Golf Federation
P.O. Box 1010
Caesarea 30660
Israel
(972) 6-361172

D'IVOIRE
(IVORY COAST)
Fédération Nationale du
Golf en Côte d'Ivoire
08 BP 1297, Abidjan 08
République de Côte
    d'Ivoire
(225) 2-13874

KENYA
Kenya Golf Union
PG Box 49609
Nairobi
Kenya
(254) 2-720074

Kenya Ladies' Golf
Union
PG Box 45615
Nairobi
Kenya

LIBYA
Libyan Golf
Federation
P.O. Box 3674
Tripoli
Libya

MALAWI
Malawi Golf Union
PG Box 1198
Blantyre
Malawi

Malawi Ladies' Golf
Union
PG 5319
Inmbe
Malawi

NIGERIA
Nigeria Amateur Golf
Association
National Sports
   Commission
P.O. Box 145
Lagos
Nigeria

MOROCCO
Federation Royale Maro-
caine de Golf
Royal Golf Rabat Dar es
   Salaam
Riute des Zaers
Rabat
Morocco

NIGERIA
Nigeria Amateur Golf
Association
P.O. Box 145
Lagos
Nigeria

SIERRA LEONE
Sierra Leone Golf Feder-
ation
Freetown Golf Club
PG Box 237
Lumley Beach
Freetown
Sierra Leone

SOUTH AFRICA
South Africa Golf Union
P.O. Box 1537
Cape Town 8000
South Africa

South African Ladies'
Golf Union
PG Box 135
1930 Vereeniging
Transvaal
South Africa

South African
Professional Golfers'
Association
PG Box 55253
Posbus Northlands
2116 Johannesburg
South Africa
(27) 011-884-3404
Fax: (27) 011-884-3436

SWAZILAND
Swaziland Golf Union
S Mabuza
P.O. Box 1739
Mbabane
Swaziland

TANZANIA
Tanzania Golf Union
PG Box 4879
Dar-es-Salaam
Tanzania

UGANDA
Uganda Golf Union
Kitante Road
PG Box 2674
Kampala
Uganda

ZAIRE
Zaire Golf Federation
Fres, Tshilombo Mwin
   Tshitol
BP 1648 Lubumbashi
Zaire

ZIMBABWE
Zimbabwe Golf
Association
P.O. Box 3327
Harare
Zimbabwe

Asia and Australasia

AUSTRALIA
Junior Golf Australia
155 Cecil Street
S. Melbourne, Victoria
Australia
(61) 03-699-7944
Fax: (61) 03-690-8510

New South Wales Golf Association
17-19 Brisbane Street
Darlinghurst, New South Wales 2010
Australia
(61) 02-264-8433
Fax: (61) 02-261-4750

Professional Golfers Association of Australia
P.O. Box 1314
41 Hume Street
Crows Nest, New South Wales 2065
Australia
(61) 439-8111
Fax: (61) 439-7888

Victorian Golf Association
15 Bardolph Street
Burwood, Victoria 3125
Australia
(61) 03-889-6731
Fax: (61) 03-889-1077

BURMA
Burma Golf Federation
c/o Aung San Stadium
Rangoon, Burma

CHINA (TAIWAN)
Golf Association of the Republic of China
71, Lane 369, Tunhua South Road
Taipei, Taiwan (106)
China

FIJI
Fiji Golf Association
P.O. Box 177
Suva
Fiji

HONG KONG
Golf Association of Hong Kong
G.P.O. Box 9978
No. 10 Yu To Sang Building
37 Queen's Road
Central
Hong Kong

INDIA
The Indian Golf Union
Tata Centre—
Third Floor
43 Chowringhee Road
Calcutta—700 071
India

INDONESIA
Indonesia Golf Association
J1. Rawanangum Muka Raya
Jakarta 13220
Indonesia

JAPAN
Japan Golf Association
606 6th Floor, Palace Building
Marunouchi,
Chiyoda-ku
Tokyo
Japan

Japan Ladies' Professional Golfers' Association
Kuranae KogyoKalkan 7E
Slanbasi 2-19-10,
Minato-ku
Tokyo
Japan
(81) 3-571-0928

Japan Professional Golf Association
Thim-Ueno Building, 4F,
1-7-15
Higashi-Ueno
Talto-Ku
Tokyo 110
Japan

Below is a summary of the original rules of golf played at St. Andrews.

1. You must tee your ball up within a club length of the hole.
2. Your tee must be upon the ground.
3. You are not to change the ball which you strike off the tee.
4. You are not to remove stones, bones, or other impediments for the sake of playing your ball, except upon the fair green and that only within a clublength of your ball.
5. If your ball lands in water, you are at liberty to take your ball out and throw it behind the hazard six yards at least; you may play it with any club, and allow your adversary a stroke for so removing your ball.
6. If your ball is found anywhere touching another one, you are to lift the first ball until you play the last.
7. At holing you are to play your ball honestly for the hole, and not to play upon your adversary's ball, not lying on your way to the hole.
8. If you should lose your ball by its being taken up or any other way, you are to go back to the spot where you struck last and drop another ball and allow your adversary a stroke for the misfortune.
9. No man at holing his ball is to be allowed to mark his way to the hole with his club or anything else.
10. If a ball is stopped by any person, horse, dog, or anything else, the ball so stopped must be played where it lies.
11. If you draw your club in order to strike and proceed so far with your stroke as to be bringing down your club, if then your club should break in any way, it is to be accounted a stroke.
12. He whose ball lies farthest from the hole is obliged to play first.
13. Neither trench, ditch, nor dike made for preservation of the links, nor the Scholars' Holes, nor the Soldiers' Lines, shall be accounted a hazard, but the ball is to be taken out, teed, and played with any iron club.

**National Golf
Foundation of Japan**
3-3-4 Sendagaya
   Shibuya-ku
Tokyo
Japan
(81) 3-3478-4355
Fax: (81) 3-3401-5867

KOREA
Korea Golf Association
Room 18-13 Floor
   Manhattan Building
36-2 Yeo Eui Do-Dong
Yeong Deung Po-Ku
Seoul
Korea
(82) 02-783-4748

MALAYSIA
**Amateur Golfers' Associ-
ation
International**
76 Ipoh Circle
Ipoh Garden
31400 Ipoh
Malaysia

**Malaysian Golf
Association**
N0. 12-A Persiaran
   Ampang
55000 Kuala Lumpur
Malaysia

NEW ZEALAND
**New Zealand Golf
Association**
65 Victoria Street,
   Box 11-824
Level 3
Wellington
New Zealand
(64) 04-472-2967
Fax: (64) 04-499-7330

**New Zealand Ladies'
Golf Union**
PG Box 13-029
Welington 4
New Zealand
(64) 04-793-868

**Professional Golfers'
Association of New
Zealand**
65 Victoria Street,
   Box 11-934
Level 3
Wellington
New Zealand
(64) 04-472-2687
Fax: (64) 04-472-2925

PAKISTAN
**Pakistan Golf
Federation**
P.O. Box 1295
Rawalpindi
Pakistan

**PAPUA
NEW GUINEA**
**Papua New Guinea
Amateur Golf
Association**
PG Box 382
Lao
Papua New Guinea

**Papua New Guinea
Ladies' Golf
Association**
PG Box 1256
Port Moresby
Papua New Guinea
(675) 21-4745

PHILIPPINES
**Republic of the
Philipines Golf
Association**
Room 200, Administrative
   Building
Rizal Memorial Sports
   Complex
Vito Cruz, Manila
Phillippines

SINGAPORE
**Singapore Golf
Association**
c/o C.L. Loong &
   Company
4 Battery Road
   No. 12-00
Bank of China Building
Singapore 0104

SRI LANKA
Ceylon Golf Union
P.O. Box 309
Model Farm Road
Colombo 8
Sri Lanka

THAILAND
Thailand Golf
Association
Railway Training Center
Vibhavadee Rangsit Road
Bangkok
Thailand

INTER-NATIONAL GOLF ASSOCIATIONS

Asia-Pacific Golf
Confederation
52, 1st Floor, Jalan Hang
Leiku 50100
Kuala Lumpur
Malaysia

European Golf
Association
En Ballgue, Casa Postale
   CH-1066
Epalinges, Lausanne
Switzerland
(41) 21-7843536
Fax: (41) 21-7843536

European PGA Tour
Wentworth Drive
Virginia Water
Surrey GU25 4LX
England
(44) 0344-842881
Fax: (44) 0344-842929

Royal and Ancient Golf
Club
St. Andrews
Fife
Scotland
(44) 0034-72112
Fax: (44) 0334-77580

South American Golf
Federation
Avda. Brasil 3025,
   Rib 50
Montevideo
Uruguay

United States Golf Association
Liberty Corner Road
Far Hills, NJ 07931
(908) 624-8400

Women Professional
Golfers' European Tour
The Tytherington Club
   Macclesfield
Cheshire SKIO 2JP
England
(44) 0625-34562
Fax: (44) 0625-611076

Beginning with the founding of golfing societies such as the Edinburgh Golfing Society (1735), the Honorable Company of Edinburgh Golfers (1744), and the Society of St. Andrews Golfers (1754), Scotland became the seat of golf as we know it today. A variety of clubs were used in the earlier days. Fashioned from wood, they consisted of a sturdy shaft with a weighted head and a padded handle, and were bound with hide from sheep, pigs, horses, or cows, or with chamois.

3

golf equipment

Around 1700, metal-headed clubs were broadly introduced as additional implements for special tasks, but eventually they took the place of some of the long-nosed wooden clubs. From this time until the middle of the nineteenth century, a golfer might carry a few long-nosed, long-shafted, straight-faced play clubs that made the ball run when hit off the tee with a flat swing. Play clubs could easily break, so most players carried reserve clubs. A grassed driver—with slightly more loft than a play club—had a slightly stiffer shaft and heavier head. It was used to give the ball more loft while maximizing distance. Three or more spoons, also wooden clubs but differing in length of shaft and degree of club-face loft, were used for dealing with various fairway lies. The baffling spoon, for example, was used to take turf with the ball and maximize lift while minimizing run. The wooden niblick, a short and well-lofted club, was used to remove the ball from bunkers and deep rough. After you finally flogged your way to the green, actually a continuation of a sandy linksland fairway, you had your trusty wooden putter to drop your featherie ball into a crude cup. At the next tee, which in the early days was adjacent to the hole but later was located adjacent to the green, you would grab a pinch of sand obtained while plucking your ball from the hole, form a sand mound, place the old featherie on the tee, and smack it with your favorite play club.

The early courses were lumpy linksland affairs such as St. Andrews and Royal Dornoch in Scotland; Royal St. George's in England; and Portmarnock, Royal Portrush, and Ballybunion in Ireland. Many of these early courses were not maintained but served as grazing land and promenades for walking. Once covered by the sea and later repositories of silt and sod from rivers running through, the linksland was sandy soil pushed into dunes and hollows by ocean winds and burrowing wildlife. Wild grasses eventually took hold; and the natural terrain, in all its wonder, became a fine obstacle course for the crude implements of golf. Although golf received early royal patronage, and had Mary Queen of Scots as an early enthusiast, it remained an informal but aristocratic game. Equipment was expensive, but it was not until 1913 that a fee was charged for playing a round on the Old Course at St. Andrews.

The craftsmanship of clubmaking evolved, and the game became a bit more ecumenical when the professional golfer came into being in the 1840s. The early professionals such as Allan Robertson, Willie Dunn, Jamie Dunn, Willie Park, and Tom Morris made their living by playing money matches, making clubs and balls, tending to the golf course, giving some instruction, and caring for the clubhouse. These professionals were low in the pecking order of the times and were not allowed to enter the clubhouse. Tom Morris, winner of the British Open in 1861, 1862, 1864, and 1867, developed from a caddie at St. Andrews to a club and ball maker under Allan Robertson. He also became a money player and longtime greenkeeper at the Royal and Ancient. The first universally respected professional, Morris broke with his mentor Allan Robertson over the gutta-percha ball, an orb made of a hard rubberlike material introduced in 1848. Robertson advocated staying with the old, more expensive and limited featherie. But Morris stood by the gutty, which ultimately made golf more accessible to the common folk. Tom developed his own gutta-percha business, but he continued to team with Robertson in matches against the Dunn brothers from Musselburgh and other competitors.

Robertson, as a clubmaker, was a pioneer in developing iron-headed clubs for specific tasks such as getting out of ruts, making precise approaches from the fairways, and hitting short pitches around the green. The arrival of the harder, heavier gutta-percha ball dramatically changed club design. The new ball, which was not of standard size or materials, was difficult to control and damaged the slender, long-nosed woods. After 1880, wooden clubheads became shorter, broader, and deeper, and the heads were no longer spliced to the shaft. New techniques, such as drilling a hole into the head of the club and inserting a tapered hickory or ash shaft, were adopted, as were other methods such as twin-splice and v-inserts. Fascinating implements such as clubs with adjustable blades or a rake mashie for playing out of rye grass or fine sand bunkers were developed. After 1900, various scoring techniques were used on clubfaces to improve ball control. A variety of clubhead inserts used on driving and fairway clubs were developed to protect the clubface from its impact with the tougher ball.

Golf bags first appeared on the market in the 1880s, and celluloid tees were introduced at the turn of the century. The sand tee gradually went the way of the dinosaur but not before a range of tee technologies including rubber tees, plastic tees, paper tees, and others were introduced. The first known patent on an artificial tee was granted in Great Britain in 1889. Dr. George Grant, one of the first African-Americans to graduate from Harvard's dental school, received, in 1899, the first U.S. patent for a golf tee that pierced the ground. Dr. Lowell, another dentist who wanted to protect his hands from grubbing in the dirt, patented his wooden tee in the 1920s and popularized it.

Club making became a true craft. The shallow-faced long-nose clubs that were prevalent from the middle of the fifteenth century gave way to new technologies inspired by the evolution of the golf ball. For example, a brass soleplate was added to wooden clubs around 1880. Craftsmen such as cabinet makers, wheelwrights, bowmakers, and others made clubs, as did golf professionals. Collectors' societies and museums have developed detailed records of clubmakers and the kinds of clubs they produced. Willie Auchterlonie, the Dunn brothers, Tom Morris, and others made wooden clubs. Irons were not used, except as utility clubs, until the gutty necessitated them. Early irons were made in only a few distinct styles, such as the cleek, lofter, sand iron, and track iron. A track iron, for example, was a small-headed club used to extract a ball from a wheel track or similar bad lie.

Until the 1890s, iron golf-club heads had been made by hand by heating the metal and hammering out a head on an anvil. When the forge technique was developed and golf became more popular, clubmakers began to mark the heads with their name or a symbol of some sort. Iron makers gradually mass-produced club-heads which were then shafted and gripped by the retailer or sold fully assembled. Eventually more easily distinguishable trademarks and names suggesting quality and craftsmanship were developed.

Competition among manufacturers spurred the development of better club-heads. Persimmon woods were introduced in the 1890s and became the material of choice when the Haskell rubber-cored ball replaced the gutta-percha. Aluminium heads were introduced at about the time Sandy Herd, playing a Haskell, defeated Harry Vardon, who played a gutty, in the 1902 British Open at Hoylake. In addition to new shafting and head technologies, the one-piece wood was developed. These were produced by Willie Dunn, Slazenger, Spalding, Mac-Gregor, and others, predominantly during the period of 1894 to 1902. Iron-headed clubs began to outnumber wooden clubs at a time when there was no limit on the number of clubs a player could use. USGA Rule 4-4 now limits the number of clubs to fourteen. One of the first sports endorsement deals occured when Harry Vardon signed on with A. G. Spalding to promote the Vardon Flyer golf ball in 1900. Vardon toured North America in a series of exhibition matches and won his only U.S. Open that year.

By the late 1940s, named clubs (such as the mashie) gave way to numbered clubs. A niblick became an 8- or 9-iron, a mashie niblick a 7-iron, a spade mashie a 6-iron, a mashie a 5-iron, and so forth. But to this day it is unlikely that a 5-iron from one set of clubs will have exactly the same loft as a 5-iron from another. And as club technology became more advanced in the twentieth century, head facings ranged from line-and-dot combinations to irregular hand-punched designs. Deep groove facings were designed to create more backspin and ball control, but after Jock Hutchinson won the 1921 British Open with them, they were outlawed. More recently, Ping, the USGA, and the PGA were involved in a legal dispute over the Tour ban on Ping's grooved clubs. The parties eventually settled out of court. Other modern manufacturers have run into conflict with golf's regulatory bodies as they continue to push the frontiers of technology.

The shapes of iron heads also changed and varied considerably at the turn of the century. Putters had bentbacks, mallet heads, hollowbacks, goosenecks, and other variations. The first center-shafted putter, the Schenectady, which was used by Walter Travis in winning the 1904 British Amateur, was banned in Britain for a number of years before it was resurrected. Manufacturers began to specialize in supplying club parts such as wooden heads, iron heads, shafts, and other components. During the modern wooden shafted era (approximately 1890–1935), Willie Park, Jr.; A. G. Spalding & Bros.; Wilson Sporting Goods; and Wright & Ditson Co. were among the leading clubmakers.

According to John M. and Morton W. Olman in their superb book *The Encyclopedia of Golf Collectibles: A Collector's Identification and Value Guide*, up until the development and acceptance of steel-shafted clubs in the late 1930s, the most noteworthy advances in the evolution of clubmaking had been the introduction of mechanization and mass production to the clubmaking industry in the late nineteenth century; the drilling of the clubhead for shaft insertion; and the idea of matched sets of clubs. Although a patent was granted for the design of a solid-steel shaft in Britain in 1894, steel-shafted clubs were not approved by the USGA until 1925 and the Royal and Ancient until 1929. The last time a major American championship was won with hickory shafts was in 1936 when Johnny Fischer won the U.S. Amateur.

In the late 1950s fiberglass shafts were marketed and Dick Mayer used fiberglass-shafted clubs to win the 1957 U.S. Open while Gary Player, an early promoter of fiberglass, won the 1965 U.S. Open with the new technology. Aluminum shafts were introduced with limited success in the 1960s; then new light-weight steel alloys and graphite shafts were adopted in the 1970s. Clubmakers continued to experiment with clubhead design, often adapting old ideas such as perimeter weighting, drilled hosels, short hosels, offset heads, and contoured soles. Cast heads made by pouring steel into molds, a method developed by Ping and other manufacturers, gained wide appeal as the sweet spot on clubheads became broader and more forgiving. In the 1980s companies like Callaway introduced and aggressively marketed oversized clubs, most notably the "Big Bertha" and other user-friendly devices. In early 1995, Nick Price signed a $25-million 10-year contract to design and endorse high-tech clubs for an obscure Cailfornia company called Atrigon Golf. At the same time some companies are now reviving "classic clubs" echoing a simpler time.

Today a purchaser of golf equipment, especially clubs, feels that he needs a degree in metallurgical engineering with a minor in physics in order to interpret terminology such as "parallax irons," "short, straight, hollow, hosel," "ballistic oversized," and "compression-molded." Competition in the equipment market is fierce, and sometimes descriptions of a product's features and claims for its benefits can be confusing. Some golfers like to assemble their own clubs from components, while others buy off the rack. Whatever your approach, you might want to have a knowledgeable professional take a look at your current equipment and assess it in terms of shaft flex, swing weight, shaft material, grip size, and other measures of fit to your physique, swing, and approach to the game. He or she can also provide you with suggestions on equipment options. Good golf schools will do the same.

Below is a very short list of some of the many equipment suppliers.

GOLF EQUIPMENT

Tommy Armour Golf
8350 North Leigh Avenue
Morton Grove, IL 60053
(708) 966-6300
(800) 723-4653

Men's apparel, bags, carryalls and luggage, balls, clubs and putters, gloves, hats, caps and visors, headcovers, umbrellas

Bridgestone Sports (U.S.A.) Inc.
15320 Industrial Park
   Boulevard N.E.
Covington, GA 30209
(404) 787-7400
(800) 358-6319

Accessories, bags, carryalls and luggage, balls, club manufacturing and repair equipment, clubs and putters, gloves, hats, caps and visors, headcovers, teaching and training aids, umbrellas

Bullet Golf
2803 S. Yale Street
Santa Ana, CA 92704
(714) 966-0310
(800) 842-3781

Apparel, bags, clubs and putters, accessories

Callaway Golf
2285 Rutherford Road
Carlsbad, CA 92008
(619) 931-177
(800) 228-2767

Bags, balls, clubs and putters, hats, caps and visors, towels, umbrellas

Cleveland Golf
5630 Cerritos Avenue
Cypress, CA 90630
(310) 630-6363
(800) 999-6263

Accessories, men's apparel,
bags, carryalls and luggage,
clubs and putters, hats,
caps and visors, headcovers, umbrellas

Cobra Golf
1812 Aston Avenue
Carlsbad, CA 92008
(619) 929-0377
(800) 223-3537

Clubs and putters

**Cubic Balance Golf
Technology**
30231 Tomas Road
Rancho Santa Margarita,
CA 92688
(714) 858-1855
(800) 727-7775

Bags, carryalls and
luggage, club manufacturing and repair
equipment, clubs and putters, gloves, shafts

**Daiwa Corporation—
Golf Division**
7421 Chapman Avenue
Garden Grove, CA 92641
(714) 895-6689
(800) 736-4653

Bags, carryalls and luggage,
clubs and putters, gloves,
headcovers

Fila Golf
5812 Machine Drive
Huntington Beach, CA
92649
(714) 897-8213
(800) 325-4399

Bags, carryalls and luggage,
clubs and putters, gloves,
hats, caps and visors

**Founders Club Golf
Company**
1780 La Costa Meadows
Drive
San Marcos, CA 92069
(619) 591-9444
(800) 654-9295

Accessories, bags, carryalls
and luggage, clubs and putters, gloves, hats, caps and
visors, headcovers, publications

H & B/Powerbilt
Box 35700
Louisville, KY 40232
(502) 585-5226
(800) 282-2287

Bags, carryalls and luggage,
clubs and putters, gloves,
hats, caps and visors, headcovers, umbrellas

Head
4801 N. 63rd Street
Boulder, CO 80301
(800) 452-4323

Accessories, apparel, clubs

Hireko Trading Company
220 Madison Way
City of Industry, CA 91746
(818) 330-5525
(800) 367-8912

Club components, clubrefinishing products and
supplies, clubs and
putters, grips, shafts

Ben Hogan Company
8000 Villa Park Drive
Richmond, VA 23228
(804) 262-3000
(800) 631-9000

Accessories, bags, carryalls
and luggage, balls, carts,
club components, clubs
and putters, gloves, grips,
hats, caps and visors, headcovers, shafts, umbrellas

Karsten Manufacturing
2201 West Desert Cove
Phoenix, AZ 85029
(602) 870-5000
(800) 528-0650

Accessories, men's apparel,
bags, carryalls and luggage,
balls, clubs and putters, display fixtures, hats, caps and
visors, headcovers, teaching
and training aids, umbrellas

Kunnan Golf
9606 Kearny Village Road
San Diego, CA 92126
(619) 271-8390
(800) 399-8599

Bags, carryalls and luggage,
carts, clubs and putters

Langert Golf Company
2774 Loker Avenue West
Carlsbad, CA 92008
(619) 438-4100
(800) 999-0333

Accessories, bags, carryalls
and luggage, clubs and putters, hats, caps and visors,
headcovers, umbrellas

Lynx Golf, Inc.
16017 East Valley Boule-
    vard
City of Industry, CA 91749
(818) 961-022
(800) 233-5969

Accessories, bags,
carryalls and luggage, clubs
and putters, gloves, hats,
caps and visors, umbrellas

**MacGregor Golf
Company**
1601 S. Slappey
    Boulevard
Albany, GA 31708
(912) 434-7000
(800) 892-7536

Bags, carryalls and
luggage, balls, clubs and
putters, gloves, hats, caps
and visors, headcovers,
rainwear and windbreakers,
umbrellas

**Maruman Golf U.S.A.,
Inc.**
5870-B Oakbrook
    Parkway
Norcross, GA 30093
(404) 446-2655
(800) 533-2716

Bags, carryalls and luggage,
clubs and putters, hats,
caps and visors, headcov-
ers, towels, umbrellas

Maxfli Golf
728 N. Pleasantburg Drive
Greenville, SC 29602
(803) 241-2000
(800) 768-4727

Accessories, bags, carryalls
and luggage, balls, clubs
and putters, gloves, hats,
caps and visors, headcov-
ers, umbrellas

Merit Golf Company
4001 Cobb International
    Boulevard
Kennesaw, GA 30144
(404) 499-1415
(800) 828-1445

Clubs and putters

**Mizuno Corporation of
America**
5125 Peachtree
    Industrial Boulevard
Norcross, GA 30092
(404) 441-5553
(800) 333-7888

Bags, carryalls and luggage,
clubs and putters, gloves,
hats, caps and visors, headcovers, rainwear and windbreakers, shoes, umbrellas

**Nicklaus Golf
Equipment**
7830 Byron Drive
West Palm Beach, FL
    33404
(407) 881-1981
(800) 322-1872

Bags, carryalls and luggage,
clubs and putters, head-
covers

Odyssey Sports
1945 Camino Vida Roble
Suite L
Carlsbad, CA 92008
(619) 431-9966
(800) 487-5664

Clubs and putters

The holes ranked the most difficult by handicap on a golf scorecard often are not the most difficult holes to par on the course. In many cases, they are the par-5 holes that a low handicap golfer can routinely par or birdie. The LPGA, PGA, and Senior Tours rank the most difficult holes to par based on stroke average during a tournament. Some of the key variables affecting these rankings are weather conditions and maintenance standards for the tournament (e.g., green speed, rough, pin placement). In 1994, the ten most difficult holes on each tour were:

LPGA TOUR

Rank	Course	Hole	Par	Yardage	Tournament
1.	Corning Country Club	1	4	402	Corning Classic
2.	Corning Country Club	13	4	412	Corning Classic
3.	Edinburgh USA	17	4	371	Edina Realty LPGA Classic
4.	Ko Olina Golf Club	18	4	377	Cup Noodles Hawaiian Ladies Open
5.	Blue Hill Country Club	1	4	417	Ping Welch's Boston
6.	Hershey Country Club (West)	13	4	388	Lady Keystone Open
7.	Columbia Edgewater Country Club	9	4	401	Ping-Cellular One Championship
8.	Eagle's Landing Country Club	15	4	406	Chick-Fil-A Charity Championship
9.	Hershey Country Club (West)	1	4	405	Lady Keystone Open
10.	Woburn Golf & Country Club	15	4	400	Weetabix Women's British Open

PGA TOUR

Rank	Course	Hole	Par	Yardage	Tournament
1.	PGA West/ Arnold Palmer Course	9	4	456	Bob Hope Chrysler Classic
2.	Oakmont Country Club	10	4	458	U.S. Open
3.	Westchester Country Club	12	4	476	Buick Classic
4.	English Turn Country Club	18	4	471	Freeport-McMoran Classic
5.	Augusta National	12	3	155	The Masters

Rank	Course	Hole	Par	Yardage	Tournament
6.	Oakmont Country Club	1	4	463	U.S. Open
7.	Pebble Beach Golf Links	9	4	464	AT&T Pebble Beach
8.	Southern Hills Country Club	2	4	458	PGA Championship
9.	Riviera Country Club	18	4	447	Nissan L.A. Open
10.	Tucson National	10	4	456	Northern Telecom

SENIOR TOUR

Rank	Course	Hole	Par	Yardage	Tournament
1.	Pinehurst No. 2	5	4	427	U.S. Senior Open
2.	PGA National Golf Club	11	4	412	PGA Seniors Championship
3.	Chester Valley Golf Club	6	4	432	Bell Atlantic Classic
4.	TPC Michigan	14	4	429	Senior Players Championship
5.	Chester Valley Golf Club	12	4	435	Bell Atlantic Classic
6.	Upper Montclair Country Club	12	4	425	Cadillac NFL Golf Classic
7.	Deerwood Club	13	4	422	Doug Sanders Classic
8.	PGA National Golf Club	15	3	164	PGA Seniors Championship
9.	Meadow Book Club	9	4	417	Northville Long Island Classic
10.	Pinehurst No. 2	18	4	415	U.S. Senior Open

Other difficult holes on great courses at home and abroad include (not in rank order):

UNITED STATES

	Course	Hole	Par	Yardage
1.	Pine Valley Golf Club (NJ)	5	3	232
2.	Cypress Point (CA)	16	3	216
3.	Merion Golf Club (East) (PA)	5	4	418
4.	Muirfield Village Golf Club (OH)	3	4	392
5.	Olympic Club (Lakeside) (CA)	4	4	438
6.	Crystal Downs Country Club (MI)	13	4	442

Course	Hole	Par	Yardage
7. Medinah Country Club (No. 3) (IL)	12	4	474
8. Seminole Golf Club (FL)	4	4	450
9. Oakland Hills Country Club (South) (MI)	18	4	447
10. Peachtree Golf Club (GA)	17	4	439
11. Quaker Ridge Golf Club (NY)	6	4	446
12. The Country Club (Open) (MA)	3	4	445
13. San Francisco Golf Club (CA)	2	4	423
14. Oak Hill Country Club (East) (NY)	1	4	447
15. Honors Course (TN)	15	4	445
16. Los Angeles Country Club (North) (CA)	5	4	478
17. Southern Hills Country Club (OK)	12	4	445
18. The Golf Club (OH)	6	4	470
19. Baltusrol Golf Club (Lower) (NJ)	4	3	194
20. Scioto Country Club (OH)	2	4	438
21. National Golf Links (NY)	10	4	450
22. Chicago Golf Club (IL)	1	4	460
23. Colonial Country Club (TX)	5	4	459
24. Spyglass Hill Golf Course (CA)	8	4	468
25. Inverness Club (OH)	7	4	452
26. Mauna Kea (HI)	11	3	247
27. Harbour Town (SC)	18	4	458
28. Bay Hill (FL)	17	3	223
29. Firestone (South Course) (OH)	16	5	625
30. Shinnecock Hills (NY)	14	4	445

INTERNATIONAL

Course	Hole	Par	Yardage
1. Muirfield (Scotland)	18	4	448
2. St. Andrews (Old) (Scotland)	17	4	461
3. Royal Birkdale (England)	6	4	468
4. Woodhall Spa (England)	9	5	560
5. Royal County Down (Ireland)	3	4	368
6. Ballybunion (Old) (Ireland)	11	4	449
7. Royal Melbourne (Composite) (Australia)	14	4	470

Course	Hole	Par	Yardage
8. Wairakei Hotel International (New Zealand)	14	5	608
9. Paraparamu Beach (New Zealand)	13	4	450
10. Banff Springs Hotel (Canada)	8	3	175
11. Royal Montreal (Blue) (Canada)	16	4	426
12. National Golf Club (Canada)	4	5	581
13. Capilano (Canada)	16	3	247
14. Durban Country Club (South Africa)	5	4	461
15. Royal Dar-es-Salam (Red) (Morocco)	9	3	199
16. Casa de Campo (Dominican Republic)	16	3	185
17. El Rincon (Colombia)	15	5	594
18. Mid-Ocean Club (Bermuda)	3	3	193
19. Club de Golf (Mexico)	8	5	562
20. Cerromar Beach Hotel Golf Club (North) (Puerto Rico)	11	3	193
21. The Jockey Club (Red) (Argentina)	13	4	440
22. Chantilly Golf Club (France)	18	5	596
23. El Saler (Spain)	9	3	160
24. Club de Golf Sotogrande (Old) (Spain)	7	4	442
25. Hirono (Japan)	15	5	555
26. Kasamigaseki (East) (Japan)	18	5	483
27. Kawana (Fuji) (Japan)	15	4	415
28. Royal Hong Kong (The New/ Eden Composite) (Hong Kong)	18	4	417
29. Royal Calcutta (India)	7	4	457
30. Bali Handura Country Club (Indonesia)	3	4	450
31. Singapore Island Country Club (Bukit Course) Singapore)	1	4	407
32. The Royal Selangor Golf Club (Malaysia)	6	4	463
33. Awana Golf and Country Club (Malaysia)	15	3	238

Gary Player
3300 PGA Boulevard
Suite 100
Palm Beach Gardens, FL
    33410
(407) 624-0300
(800) 475-2937

Apparel, clubs and
putters, gloves

Prince Golf
1208 Tappan Circle
Carrolton, TX 75006
(800) 999-0333

Clubs, balls, and
accessories

Progear, Inc.
14850 Woodham Drive
Suite B-135
Houston, TX 77073
(713) 821-4200
(800) 845-4327

Bags, clubs and putters,
gloves, hats, caps and visors

Progroup, Inc.
6201 Mountain View Road
Ooltewah, TN 37363
(615) 238-5890
(800) 735-6300

Apparel, men's bags,
carryalls and luggage, clubs
and putters, hats, caps and
visors, headcovers, rain-
wear and windbreakers,
towels

Pro Select
951 N. Larch
Elmhurst, IL 60126
(800) 233-6489

Clubs and putters

Ram Golf Corporation
2020 Indian Boundary
    Drive
Melrose Park, IL 60160
(708) 681-5800
(800) 833-4653

Accessories, apparel, men's
bags, carryalls and luggage,
balls, clubs and putters,
computer systems and software, crests and emblems,
gloves, grips, hats, caps and
visors, headcovers, rain-
wear and windbreakers,
range equipment, towels,
umbrellas

Rawlings Golf
20301 Nordhof Street
Chatsworth, CA 91311
(818) 349-3164
(800) 443-8222

Bags, carryalls and
luggage, clubs and
putters

**Ryobi-Toski
Corporation**
160 Essex Street
Newark, OH 43055
(614) 345-9683
(800) 848-2075

Bags, carryalls and luggage,
club components, clubs
and putters, grips, hats,
caps and visors, headcov-
ers, shafts

Slazenger Golf, U.S.A.
25 Draper Street
Brandon Mill Complex
Suite 202
Greenville, SC 29611
(803) 295-4444
(800) 766-2615

Accessories, apparel, men's
bags, carryalls and luggage,
clubs and putters, gloves,
hats, caps and visors, headcovers

Slotline Golf
5252 McFadden Avenue
Huntington Beach, CA
    92649
(714) 898-2888
(800) 854-8169

Clubs and putters

**Spalding Sports World-
wide**
425 Meadow Street
Chicopee, MA 10121
(413) 536-1200
(800) 642-5004

Bags, carryalls and
luggage, balls, clubs
and putters

Square Two Golf
18 Gloria Lane
Fairfield, NJ 07004
(201) 227-7783
(800) 526-2250

Bags, carryalls and
luggage, balls, clubs
and putters, gloves, hats,
caps and visors, head-
covers, umbrellas

**Taylor Made Golf Com-
pany, Inc.**
2271 Cosmos Court
Carlsbad, CA 92009
(619) 931-1991
(800) 456-8633

Men's apparel, bags,
carryalls and luggage, clubs
and putters, gloves, hats,
caps and visors, hardcovers,
rainwear and windbreakers,
umbrellas

**Stan Thompson Golf
Club Company**
2616 Temple Heights
　Drive
Oceanside, CA 92056
(619) 630-2660
(800) 959-5900

Clubs and putters

Tiger Shark Golf, Inc.
4235 Ponderosa Avenue
San Diego, CA 92123
(619) 292-4653
(800) 654-9892

Bags, carryalls and luggage,
club components, clubs
and putters, grips, hats,
caps and visors, headcov-
ers, towels, umbrellas

**Titleist and Footjoy
Worldwide**
333 Bridge Street
Fairhaven, MA 02719
(508) 979-2000
(800) 225-8500

Balls, shoes, clubs and putters, gloves, bags, carryalls
and luggage, socks and
peds, accessories, carts

**Wilson Sporting Goods
Co.**
8700 W. Bryn Mawr
　Avenue
Chicago, IL 60631
(312) 714-6400
(800) 622-0444

Men's apparel, bags,
carryalls and luggage, balls,
clubs and putters, gloves,
grips, hats, caps and visors,
headcovers, rainwear and
windbreakers, umbrellas

Wood Brothers Golf
200A North Houston
　Avenue
Box 1388
Humble, TX 77347
(713) 446-0445
(800) 800-8424

Clubs and putters, hats,
caps and visors, head-
covers, shafts

Yonex Corporation
3520 Challenger Street
Torrance, CA 90503
(310) 542-8111
(800) 449-6639

Accessories, bags, carryalls
and luggage, clubs and putters, gloves, hats, caps and
visors, headcovers, towels,
umbrellas

Zett U.S.A., Inc.
200 S. Cypress Street
Orange, CA 92666
(714) 639-9850
(800) 622-7007

Accessories, bags, carryalls
and luggage, clubs and putters, gloves, hats, caps and
visors, headcovers

There seems to be no end of theory on golf in–struction, ranging from mental gymnastics in the zen tradition as expressed in *Golf in the Kingdom* and other books to more orthodox instructional techniques that deal with muscle memory and the mechanics of the game. Your local club or driving range could very well have a golf instructor and practice venue that is appropriate for you. Or you might want to take a golf getaway vacation to a resort or golf-course real-estate rental that has elaborate practice facilities and a swing school to cure the real or imagined ills of your game.

With the advent of more sophisticated instructional techniques, it is easier to recognize one's swing tendencies and correct faults with the help of a good instructor. As with any self-improvement endeavor, it would be helpful to do your own needs assessment to honestly evaluate the current state of your game, your commitment (in time and money) to golf, and realistic goals that are attainable based on your abilities, dedication, time, and resources.

A good golf instructor can help you with this assessment, but it is most important to "know thyself" before you look for a magic formula to improve your golf game. One of the more frustrating obstacles for true golf instructors is their inability to develop an ongoing program with

4

golf schools

a pupil that will build his or her golf game over a period of time. There has to be a meeting of the minds and styles of both student and teacher before real progress can be made.

Golf instructional programs come in many forms such as one-to-one instruction and group lessons. Specialized programs such as women's golf schools and instruction based on specific swing schools of thought are available. There are also a variety of programs for junior golfers and those who have taken up the game at an advanced age.

Some professionals, such as Lee Trevino, claim to have never had golf instruction. Others travel with an entourage including a swing doctor, sports psychologist, caddie, agent, and other personnel of the modern Tour support system.

After assessing your own golf needs and while shopping for golf instruction, you should ask yourself these basic questions:

- What are the strengths and weaknesses of my game?
- What kind of instruction program will best meet my golf needs, for example, self-instruction from books, magazines, videotapes, and other sources, or a structured program?
- How much time and money can I devote to this effort?
- What are my short- and long-term golf goals, and what is a realistic timetable for reaching them?
- How am I going to monitor my progress and make adjustments over a period of time?
- Why do I play golf, and how does my instructional program fit into the scheme of things?

A goal for a middle-aged high handicapper with little time to work on his or her game might be to get a complete game assessment in order to identify basic tendencies in the grip, stance, address, equipment selection, and golf habits that can be readily improved. Short term, the goal might be to play a respectable game in the 90s that can be improved when more time becomes available. Low handicappers might want to work on specific weaknesses such as the game from 150 yards in, sand wedges, or putting. A golf professional or golf school can help you to diagnose your game and develop a practice program that fits your needs.

A good golf instructor will question you in detail about your golf equipment, game, needs, and goals. A written and possibly a video record will be made of your tendencies on a practice tee or on the course. A group or individual program will be arranged for you. Golf schools have programs that have been refined based on hundreds of hours of instruction. Before entering these programs make certain you undertand the teaching philosophy, the techniques used, the amount of time spent in each of the sessions, the student-teacher ratios, the nature of the practice facilities, access to the golf course and practice facilities during non-teaching hours, instructional materials provided, equipment assessment techniques, staff credentials, and references. If a significant time and financial commitment is required, you might want to contact golfers who have previously attended the school.

Below is a selected short list of golf schools, many of which have programs at more than one location. You also might want to contact the PGA or LPGA for its list of master teachers and find out their criteria for levels of instructional ability in their teaching and certification program. Publications such as *Golf* magazine regularly list the top instructors. Many of the instructors on these recommended lists have written books, developed instructional videos, and started golf schools. For example, *Golf*'s "50 Top Teachers in America" list includes Peggy Kirk Bell, Fred Griffen, Rick Smith, David Leadbetter, and other outstanding teachers.

One of the best books available on golf schools is *Golf Schools: The Complete Guide* by Barbara Wolf and Zelda Kaplan (First Person Press, $14.95, 192 pages; 25 Allen Road, Swampscott, MA 01907). This reference provides a good survey of more than four hundred golf schools for adults and juniors as well as special-interest programs and associations for women, the physically challenged, collegians, and other groups.

GOLF SCHOOLS

Adult

ALABAMA

Chuck Hogan Golf Schools
4880 Valleydale Road
Birmingham, AL
  35242-9981
(205) 991-3673
(800) 345-4245

Schools held at the Sedona Golf Resort in Sedona, Arizona and Birmingham, Alabama; and at golf clubs and resorts in Dallas, Texas; Braynard, Minnesota; Pebble Beach, California; Tempe, Arizona; and Waikaloa, Hawaii

ARIZONA

Golf Schools of Scottsdale
4949 East Lincoln Drive
Suite 102
Scottsdale, AZ 85253
(602) 998-4800
(800) 356-6678

Schools held at La Posada Resort, Scottsdale, Arizona; Denver and Colorado Springs, Colorado; and Lake Havasu, Arizona

John Jacob's Practical Golf Schools
7825 East Redfield Road
Suite E
Scottsdale, AZ
  85260-6977
(800) 472-5007
Fax: (602) 991-8243

Schools held at Marriott's Grand Hotel and Resort, Point Clear, Alabama; The Wigwam Resort, Litchfield Park, Arizona; Painted Mountain Golf Club, Mesa, Arizona; Marriott's Mountain Shadows Resort/Camelback Golf Club, Scottsdale, Arizona; Marriott's Fairfield Inn/Camelback Golf Club, Scottsdale, Arizona; Tucson National Golf & Conference Resort, Tucson, Arizona; Chardonnay Club/Inn at Napa Valley, Napa, California; Marriott's Desert Springs Resort and Spa, Palm Desert, California; Marriott's Rancho Las Palmas Resort, Rancho Mirage, California; Skyland Mountain Golf Resort, Crested Butte, Colorado; The Bonaventure Resort and Spa, Fort Lauderdale, Florida; Marriott's Orlando World Center, Orlando,

Florida; Marriott's Marco Island Resort & Golf Club, Marco Island, Florida; Grand Harbor Golf & Beach Club, Vero Beach, Florida; Grand Traverse Resort, Traverse City, Michigan; Marriott's Tan-Tar-A Resort, Golf Club & Spa, Osage Beach, Missouri; Angel Park Golf Club, Las Vegas, Nevada; Marriott's Seaview Resort, Absecon, New Jersey; Hanah Country Inn, Margaretville, New York; Marriott's Wind Watch Hotel & Golf Club, Hauppage, Long Island, New York; Langdon Farms, Aurora, Oregon; Rancho Viejo Resort, Rancho Viejo, Texas; Homestead Resort, Midway, Utah; Lake Lawn Lodge, Delavan, Wisconsin; Jackson Hole Golf & Tennis Club/Worth Hotel, Jackson, Wyoming

Gary McCord/Peter Kostis Golf School
Gray Hawk Golf Club
19800 Pima Road
Scottsdale, AZ 85255
(602) 502-1800

Schools held on-site

CALIFORNIA

Doral Golf Learning Center
Golf Academy at Aviara
Aviara Golf Club
7447 Batiquitos Drive
Carlsbad, CA 92009
(619) 438-4539
(800) 433-7468

Schools held on-site

The Golf Clinic at Pebble Beach
Box 1129
Pebble Beach, CA 93953
(408) 624-5421
(800) 321-9401

Schools held at Poppy Hills, Pebble Beach, and Spyglass; programs also held at The Royal Waikoloan in Hawaii

The Golf University at San Diego
17550 Bernardo Oaks Drive
San Diego, CA 92128
(619) 485-8880
(800) 426-0966

Schools held at Rancho Bernardo Inn; play available on-site and at nearby courses

Riley School of Golf
P.O. Box 3695
Palm Desert, CA 92261
(619) 341-1009
(800) 847-4539

Schools held at Desert Princess Country Club, Palm Desert, California; Wild Wing Plantation, Myrtle Beach, South Carolina

COLORADO

Academy of Golf at the Broadmoor
Broadmoor Resort
1 Lake Avenue
Colorado Springs, CO 80906
(800) 832-6235

Schools held at the resort

Craft-Zavichas Golf Schools
600 Dittmer Avenue
Pueblo, CO 81005
(719) 564-4449
(800) 858-9633

Schools held at the Pueblo West Golf Club in Pueblo, Colorado; at the Shanty Creek Resort in Bellaire, Michigan; and at the Matanzas Golf Course at the Sheraton Palm Coast Golf & Tennis Resort in Florida

CONNECTICUT

Golf Digest Instruction Schools
Box 395
Turnbull, CT 06611
(203) 373-7130
(800) 243-6121

Schools held at Troon North Golf Club, North Scottsdale, AZ; Pala Mesa Resort, San Diego, California; Quail Lodge Resort and Golf Club, Carmel, California; Rancho La Quinta Golf Club, La Quinta (Palm Springs); Sonnenalp Resort, Vail, Colorado; Innisbrook Hilton Resort, Tarpon Springs (Tampa) Florida; Chateau Elan Golf Club, Braselton (Atlanta), Georgia; Cloister and Sea Island Club, Sea Island, Georgia; Sun Valley Resort, Sun Valley, Idaho; Pine Meadow Golf and Country Club, Mundelein (Chicago), Illinois; Sunriver Resort, Bend, Oregon; Williamsburg Inn, Colonial Williamsburg, Virginia

FLORIDA

The Academy of Golf at PGA National
PGA National Golf Club
1000 Avenue of
   Champions
Palm Beach Gardens, FL
   33418
(407) 627-7593
(800) 832-6235

Schools held at the resort

Jimmy Ballard Golf Workshop
Palm Beach Polo and
Country Club
11809 Polo Club Road
West Palm Beach, FL
   33414
(407) 798-7233 (Florida)
(803) 837-3000 (Hilton
   Head, SC)

Schools held at the
Jacaranda Golf Club and
Hilton Head National Golf
Course

Howie Barrow School of Golf at Grenelefe
Grenelefe Resort and
   Conference Center
3200 State Road 546
Grenelefe, FL 33844
(813) 422-7511
(800) 282-7875

Schools held at the
Grenelefe Resort

Doral Resort and Country Club
4400 Northwest 87 Avenue
Miami, FL 33178-2192
(800) 72-DORAL

Schools held at the resort

Florida Golf School/America's Favorite Golf Schools
3703 North A1A
Suite D
Fort Pierce, FL 34949
(407) 464-3706
(800) 365-6727

Schools held in six Florida locations: Clearwater, Pompano Beach, Lehigh, Orlando, Naples, and Palm Coast. Also administers America's Favorite Golf Schools in Sedona, Arizona; Los Angeles, California; San Diego, California; Santa Rosa, California; Colorado Springs, Colorado; Littleton, Colorado; Mystic, Connecticut; Destin, Florida; Fort Myers, Florida; Naples, Florida; Orlando, Florida; Port Charlotte, Florida; Port St. Lucie, Florida; Pompano Beach, Florida; St. Augustine, Florida; Atlanta, Georgia; Chicago, Illinois; Findlay, Illinois; Las Vegas, Nevada; Gettysburg, Pennsylvania; Beaufort, South Carolina; Myrtle Beach, South Carolina; Houston, Texas; San Antonio, Texas; and Rochester, Vermont.

Al Frazzini's Golf Course
Quail Hollow Country
   Club
6225 Old Pasco Road
Wesley Chapel, FL 33544
(904) 532-1112
(800) 598-8127

Schools held on-site

The Golf School
Plantation Inn and
   Golf Resort
Box 1116
Crystal River, FL 32629
(904) 795-4211
(800) 240-2555 (in FL)
(802) 464-4184
(800) 240-2555 (in VT
   and MD)

Schools held at the
Plantation Inn, Mount
Snow, Vermont, and Ocean
City, Maryland

The Grand Cypress Resort Academy of Golf
One North Jacaranda
Orlando, FL 32836
(407) 239-1975
(800) 835-7377

Schools held at the 3-hole custom-designed practice facility within the resort

Heritage Golf Schools
1089 W. Morse Boulevard
Suite C
Winter Park, FL 32789
(407) 628-5818
(800) 362-1469

Schools held at Silverado Country Club and Resort, Napa, California; LaQuinta (Citrus Course), California; Kiawah Island Inn & Villas, South Carolina; Woodlands Resort-TPC at The Woodlands, Texas

Innisbrook Golf Institute
Innisbrook Hilton Resort
and Country Club
P.O. Drawer 1088
Tarpon Springs, FL 34688
(813) 942-2000
(800) 456-2000

Schools held at the resort

David Leadbetter Golf Academy
Quail West Golf and
Country Club
6303 Burnham Road
Naples, FL 33999
(813) 592-1444

Schools held at Quail West; Lake Nona Golf Course, Orlando, Florida; PGA West, LaQuinta, California

Nicklaus-Flick Golf Schools
11780 U.S. Highway One
North Palm Beach, FL
33408
(800) 642-5528

Schools held at Desert Mountain, Scottsdale, Arizona; Pebble Beach Resort, California; Ibis Golf and Country Club, Palm Beach Gardens, Florida; and Boyne Highlands Resort, Harbor Springs, Michigan

Arnold Palmer Golf Academy
9000 Bay Hill Boulevard
Orlando, FL
32819-4899
(407) 876-2429
(800) 523-5999

Schools held at Arnold Palmer's Bay Hill Club, Orlando, Florida; Saddlebrook Resort, Wesley Chapel, Florida; Oasis Resort, Mesquite, Nevada

Paradise Golf Schools
975 Imperial Golf Course
Boulevard
Naples, FL 33942
(813) 592-0204
(800) 624-3543

Schools held at Golden Gate Country Club, Naples, Florida; Marco Shores, Marco Island, Florida

Bill Skelley's Schools of Golf
1847 East John Sims Parkway
Niceville, FL 32578
(904) 729-3110
(800) 541-7707

Schools held at Gold Canyon Ranch, Apache Junction (Phoenix), Arizona; Bluewater Bay Resort, Niceville, Florida; Mission Inn Golf and Tennis Resort, Howey-in-the-Hills (Orlando), Florida; Fairfield Glade Resort, Crossville, Tennessee

**United States Senior
Golf Academy**
1300 Country Club Drive
N.E. Palm Bay, FL 32905
(407) 729-9717
(800) 654-5752

**Ken Venturi Golf Train-
ing Centers**
The Marketplace
Suite 72
7600 Dr. Phillips
    Boulevard
Orlando, FL 32819
(407) 352-9669
fax (407) 352-9270

Schools held at Old South
Golf Links, Hilton Head
Island, South Carolina

ILLINOIS

**Eagle Ridge Golf Acad-
emy**
U.S. Route 20, Box 777
444 Eagle Ridge Drive
Galena, IL 61036
(815) 777-2444
(800) 892-2269

Schools held at Eagle Inn
and Resort

INDIANA

**United States
Golf Academy**
Swan Lake Golf Resort
5203 Plymouth-LaPorte
    Trail
Plymouth, IN 46563
(219) 935-5680
(800) 582-7539

Schools held at Swan Lake
Golf Resort

MICHIGAN

Boyne Golf Schools
Boyne Mountain Resort
Boyne Mountain Road
Boyne Falls, MI 49713
(800) GO-BOYNE

Schools held at the resort

**Treetops Sylvan Resort
Golf Schools**
Treetops Sylvan Resort
3962 Wilkinson Road
Gaylord, MI 49735
(517) 732-6711
(800) 444-6711

Schools held at the resort

NEW YORK

**The Roland Stafford
Golf School**
P.O. Box 81
Arkville, NY 12406
(914) 586-3187
(800) 447-8894

Schools held at the Grand
Palms Golf and Country
Club, Pembroke Pines,
Florida; Perdido Bay
Resort, Pensacola, Florida;
Tory Pines Resort,
Francestown, New Hamp-
shire; Peek'n Peak Resort,
Clymer, New York,
Christman's Windham
House, Windham,
New York; Hotel l'Esterel,
Quebec (Canada);
Mount Mansfield Resort,
Stowe, Vermont

NORTH CAROLINA

**Bertholy-Method
Golf School**
Box 406
Foxfire Village, NC 27281
(919) 281-3093

Schools held at the 6-acre
practice area adjacent to
the 36-hole Foxfire
Country Club

**Pine Needles
Golf School**
Box 88
Southern Pines, NC 28387
(919) 692-7111

Schools held at the Pine
Needles Resort.

Pinehurst Golf Advantage School
Pinehurst Resort and
Country Club
Pinehurst, NC 28374
(910) 295-6811
(800) 795-4653

Schools held at the resort

Woodlake Golf Schools
Woodlake Country Club
P.O. Box 648
Woodlake Vass, NC 28394
(800) 334-1126

Schools held on-site

SOUTH CAROLINA

The Phil Ritson Golf School
Pawleys Plantation Golf
   and Country Club
Highway 17, Box 2580
Pawleys Island, SC 29585
(803) 237-4993
(800) 624-4653

Schools held at Pawleys
Plantation; Brunswick
Plantation, Calabash,
North Carolina; Deer
Creek, Overland Park,
Kansas

Vintage Golf Schools
Box 5045
Hilton Head Island, SC
   29938
(803) 681-2406

Schools held on-site

TEXAS

The Academy of Golf Dynamics
45 Club Estates Parkway
Austin, TX 78738
(512) 261-3300,
(800) 879-2008

Schools held at the Kissing
Camels Club, Colorado
Springs, Colorado; Hills of
Lakeway, Austin

Barton Creek Golf Advantage School
Barton Creek Resort
8212 Barton Club Drive
Austin, TX 78735
(512) 329-4000
(800) 336-6157

Schools held at the resort

Byron Nelson Golf School
Four Seasons
   Resort and Club
4150 North MacArthur
   Boulevard
Irving, TX 75038
(214) 717-0700
(800) 322-3442

Schools held at the resort

Dave Peltz Short-Game School
1200 Lakeway Drive
Suite 21
Austin, TX 78734
(512) 261-6493
(800) 833-7370

Schools held at Boca Raton
Resort and Club, Boca
Raton, Florida; PGA West,
LaQuinta, California

Harvey Penick Golf Academy at Golfsmith International
11000 I-H North
Austin, TX 78753
(800) 477-5869

Schools held at Golfsmith's
41-acre site

VERMONT

Mountain Top Golf School
Mountain Top Inn
   and Resort
Mountain Top Road
Chittenden, VT 05737
(802) 483-2311
(800) 445-2100

School held at Mountain
Top Inn and Resort

MINORITY GOLF SCHOLARSHIPS

The Chrysler Junior Golf Scholarship Program offers annual grants of $1,000 to deserving students ages twelve to eighteen who have submitted applications; personal essays; and parent, teacher, and/or mentor recommendations. The program is operated in conjunction with the American Junior Golf Association. Forty winners were announced in 1994, the first year of the program; and the recipients ranged from ranked state champions to recreational golfers.

For more information, contact: Bill Dickey, President, National Minority Junior Golf Scholarship Association, 1140 E. Washington St., Suite 102, Phoenix, AZ 85034, (602) 258-7851.

**Natural Asset
Golf Program**
Stoweflake Inn
   and Resort
Box 369, Mountain Road
Stowe, VT 05672
(802) 253-7355

Schools held at Stowe
Country Club

**The Original
Golf School**
Mount Snow Resort
Route 100
West Dover, VT 05356
(802) 464-7788
(800) 451-4211

Schools held at Mount
Snow; Crystal River,
Florida; River Run, Ocean
City, Maryland; and Sugar-
loaf Resort, Carabassett,
Maine

VIRGINIA

Wintergreen Golf Academy
Wintergreen Resort
P.O. Box 706
Wintergreen, VA 22958
(804) 325-2200
(800) 325-2200

Schools held at the resort

Junior

Each school has its own policy on age groups served; the general range is from ages seven to eighteen. Some schools are coed; others only take boys or girls.

ALABAMA

**Crimson Tide
Golf Academy**
Box 40405
Tuscaloosa, AL 35404
(205) 752-0675

ALASKA

**Elmendorf Junior
Golf Clinic**
Elmendorf
   Air Force Base
Eagle Glen Golf Course
Elmendorf AFB, AK 99506
(907) 552-3821

ARIZONA

**Arizona State
University Golf
Academy**
Arizona State University
306 ICA Building
Tempe, AZ 85287
(602) 965-3262

**Exceller Programs Golf
Schools**
7500 East Butherus
Scottsdale, AZ 85260
(602) 998-1038
(800) 424-7438

**John Jacobs Practical
Golf Schools**
Marriott's Camelback Golf
    Club
7847 Mockingbird Lane
Scottsdale, AZ 85253
(800) 24-CAMEL

CALIFORNIA

**Billy Casper's Hall of
Fame Golf Camp**
32 Washington Avenue
Port Richmond, CA 94801
(415) 215-1000

**Nike Junior
Golf Camps**
919 Sir Francis Drake
    Boulevard
Kentfield, CA
    94904-4002
(415) 459-0459
(800) 6453226

Camps at twenty college,
prep school, and club sites
in U.S.

**Northern California PGA
Resident School**
3645 Fulton Avenue
Sacramento, CA 95821
(916) 481-4506

**Stanford University Golf
Camp**
Stanford University
c/o U.S. Sports
    Development
919 Sir Francis Drake
    Boulevard
Kentfield, OH 94904
(800) 433-6060

**The Ultimate Junior
Golf Clinic**
P.O. Box 1129
Pebble Beach, CA 93953
(800) 321-9401

COLORADO

**Colorado Section Junior
Golf Academy**
Colorado Section PGA
12323 East Cornell Avenue
Aurora, CO 80014
(303) 745-3697

**Falcon Junior
Golf Academy**
U.S. Air Force Academy
Colorado Springs, CO
    80840
(719) 472-1895
(800) 666-8723

CONNECTICUT

**Golf Digest Junior
Instruction Schools**
Box 395
Trumbull, CT 06611
(800) 243-6121

FLORIDA

**Fellowship of
Christian Athletes Golf
Camp**
Box 664
Ponte Vedra Beach, FL
    32004
(904) 273-9541

Gator Golf Camp
Box 2313
Gainesville, FL 32602
(904) 375-4683

**Innisbrook Junior
Golf Institute**
Box 1088
Tarpon Springs, FL 34688
(813) 942-2000
(800) 942-2000

**David Leadbetter
Golf Academy Junior
Golf School**
Quail West Golf and
   Country Club
6303 Burnham Road
Naples, FL 33999
(813) 592-1444

Osprey Golf Camp
University of North
   Florida Athletics
4567 St. Johns Bluff Road
   South
Jacksonville, FL 32224
(904) 646-2535

**Arnold Palmer
Golf Academy**
Bay Hill Club
9000 Bay Hill Boulevard
Orlando, FL 32819
(407) 876-2429
(800) 523-5999

**PGA National Junior
Golf Academies**
1000 Avenue of
   Champions
Palm Beach Gardens, FL
   33418
(407) 627-7593
(800) 832-6235

**PGA Junior
Golf Schools**
Box 109601
Palm Beach Gardens, FL
   33410
(407) 624-8456

**Ron Philos
Golf School**
Amelia Island Plantation
P.O. Box 3000
Amelia Island, FL 32035
(800) 874-6878

GEORGIA

**Georgia Junior Golf
Foundation Academy**
Georgia Junior Golf Foun-
   dation
121 Village Parkway
Building 3
Marietta, GA 30067
(404) 955-4272
(800) 949-4742

**Georgia Southern
University Golf Camp**
L.B. 8082
Statesboro, GA 30460
(912) 681-9100

ILLINOIS

**Eagle Ridge
Golf Academy**
Eagle Ridge Inn
   and Resort
U.S. Route 20, Box 777
Galena, IL 61036
(815) 777-2444
(800) 892-2269

**Illinois State
University Golf Camp**
Illinois State University
7130 Horton Field House
Normal, IL 61761
(309) 438-3635

**University of Illinois
Summer Camp**
University of Illinois
113 Assembly Hall
1800 South First Street
Champaign, IL 61820
(217) 244-7278

INDIANA

**Sam Carmichael's Junior
Golf School**
Indiana University
Assembly Hall
Bloomington, IN 47405
(812) 855-7950

**Purdue University Boys'
and Girls'
Golf Camps**
Purdue University
1586 Stewart Center
Room 110
West Lafayette, IN 47907
(317) 494-3216

IOWA

**Cyclone Country
Golf Camp**
Iowa State University
Box 1995
Ames, IA 50010
(515) 232-3999

Cyclone Golf Academy
Iowa State University
Strange Road
Ames, IA 50011
(515) 294-6727

**Iowa Section PGA Junior
Golf Acadenmy**
University of Northern
  Iowa
c/o Golf Academy,
  PGA of America,
  Iowa Section
1930 St. Andrews, N.E.
Cedar Rapids, IA 52402
(319) 378-9142

KANSAS

**Girls' Jayhawk
Golf Camp**
904 Prescott Drive
Lawrence, Kansas 66044
(913) 842-6724

Jayhawk Golf Camp
2104 Inverness Drive
Lawrence, Kansas 66047
(913) 842-1907
(913) 842-1714

Shocker Golf Camp
Wichita State University
Campus 18
Wichita, KS 67208
(316) 689-3257

KENTUCKY

**Kentucky Section PGA
Junior Golf Academy**
Kentucky Section PGA
  Junior Golf Academy
P.O. Box 18396
Louisville, KY 40261
(502) 499-7255

**Murray State
University Golf School**
305 Sparks Hall
Murray State University
Murray, KY 42071
(502) 762-2187

LOUISIANA

**Southern Junior
Golf Acadeny**
4008 Irvine Street
Baton Rouge, LA 70808
(504) 383-8714

MAINE

**Sugarloaf Junior
Golf Camp**
Sugarloaf Golf Club
  and School
The Sugarloaf Inn
Carrabassett Valley, ME
  04947
(800) THE-LOAF

MARYLAND

**Ronnie Scales
Golf Camp**
University of Maryland
  Golf Course
College Park, MD 20740
(301) 403-4299

MASSACHUSETTS

**Crumpin-Fox
Junior Camps**
Crumpin-Fox Golf Club
Parmenter Road
Bernardston, MA 01337
(413) 648-9101

GOLF HEAD TRIP

The Golf Academy of Hilton Head Island is offering a serious Junior Masters Program for the equally serious price of just under $30,000. The program is offered to high-school-age youths with single-digit handicaps who intend to pursue golf in college. A four-year high school curriculum is offered, but more abbreviated courses of study may be pursued. The program is headed by Class A PGA instructor John Daniel and operates out of the Port Royal and Shipyard Courses at Hilton Head. SAT preparation, college and scholarship services, and assistance in the application process are included. Students are housed at the Collages Resort, a gated community located in the Shipyard Plantation.

For more information, contact: Junior Masters Program, Golf Academy of Hilton Head Island, P.O. Box 5580, Hilton Head Island, SC 29938, (800) 925-0467, (803) 785-4540.

MICHIGAN

Ferris Golf Camp
Ferris State University
Lifelong Learning, Alumni
    Building 226
410 Oak Street
Big Rapids, MI 49307
(616) 592-3808

**Michigan State
University,
Sports Camps**
222 Jenison Fieldhouse
East Lansing, MI 48824
(517) 355-5264

**University of Michigan
Golf Camp of
Champions**
1000 South State Street
Ann Arbor, MI 48109
(313) 998-7239

MINNESOTA

**Rob Hary Junior
Golf School**
6300 Auto Club
    Boulevard
Bloomington, MN 55438
(612) 884-2409

Minnesota Golf Instructional Camp
University of Minnesota
3812 Moccasin Court
Burnsville, MN 55337
(612) 625-5863

**Minnesota PGA
Junior Golf Academy**
Bunker Hills Golf Club
Highway 242
Foley Boulevard
Coon Rapids, MN 55433

MISSISSIPPI

Ole Miss Golf Camp
Center for
    Continuing Studies
Box 879
University of Mississippi
University, MS 38677
(601) 232-7241

NEW MEXICO

**Sun Country Section
PGA Junior Academy**
111 Cardenas Northeast
Albuquerque, NM 87108
(505) 260-0167

NEW YORK

Kutsher's Sports Academy
Monticello, NY 12701
(914) 794-5400
(800) 724-0238

Pepsi Met PGA Golf School
Box 268
Wykagyl Station, NY
   10804
(914) 235-0312

NORTH CAROLINA

Bertholy Method Golf Schools
Foxfire Village, NC 27281
(919) 281-3093

Campbell University Golf School
Box 10
Buies Creek, NC 27506
(919) 893-4111

Duke University Golf School
Route 751 at Science Drive
Durham, NC
   27708-0551
(919) 681-2494
(919) 493-1517

Elon College Golf School
Elon College Athletic
   Department
Elon College, NC 27244
(910) 584-2420

Jack Lewis Golf Camp
Wake Forest University
Box 7567
Winston-Salem, NC 27109
(910) 759-6000

North Carolina State University Golf School
3000 Ballybunion Way
Raleigh, NC 27613
(919) 846-1536

Pine Needles Youth Camp
Box 88
Southern Pines, NC 28374
(800) 634-9297

Pinehurst Junior Golf Advantage Schools
Box 4000
Pinehurst Hotel and Country Club
Pinehurst, NC 28374
(800) 634-9297

University of North Carolina Golf School
Box 4402
Chapel Hill, NC 27515
(919) 962-2211

OHIO

Fighting Scot Golf Camp
College of Wooster
Wooster, OH 44691
(216) 263-2170

OKLAHOMA

Mike Holder's Cowboy Golf Camp
Gallagher-Iba Arena
Stillwater, OK 74078
(405) 377-4289

South Central PGA Junior Golf Academy
Oklahoma Central State
   University
c/o South Central
   PGA Section
2745 East Skelly
   No. 103
Tulsa, OK 74105
(918) 742-5672

PENNSYLVANIA

JKST Golf School
Haverford College
c/o JKST, Inc.
696 Raven Road
Wayne, PA 19087
(215) 293-0678

Kiski Golf School
1888 Brett Lane
Saltsburg, PA 15681
(412) 639-3586

**Penn State
Golf Camps**
Penn State University
409 Keller Building
University Park, PA 16802
(814) 865-0561

**Philadelphia PGA Junior
Golf Academy**
Penn State University
410 Keller Conference
    Center
University Park, PA 16802
(814) 865-6231

SOUTH CAROLINA

**Junior Golf Academy at
Furman University**
3300 Poinsett Highway
Greenville, SC 29613
(803) 294-9091

TENNESSEE
**Tennessee Golf
Academy**
4711 Trousdale Drive
Nashville, TN 37220
(615) 833-9689

**Tennessee PGA Junior
Golf Academy**
1500 Legends
    Club Lane
Franklin, TN 37064
(615) 790-7600

TEXAS

**Texas A&M
Golf School**
c/o Athletic Department
Texas A&M
College Station, TX 77843
(409) 845-4533

**Texas Tech Junior Golf
Academy**
Box 4070
Lubbock, TX 79409
(806) 742-3335

WISCONSIN

**Silver Sands
Golf School**
South Shore Drive
Delavan, WI 53115
(414) 728-6120

International Golf Schools

**The Ayrshire
Golf Agency**
Golfing Holidays
    for Juniors
P. O. Box 54
Ayr, Scotland
(44) 292 570067
Fax: (44) 292 570888

Five five-day sessions in
July and August for golfers
ages ten to eighteen.
Courses played include
Fullurton, Seafield, Girvan,
Dalmilling, and others in
Scotland

**Peter Bullingall
Golf Schools**
Barnham Broom Hotel,
Golf and Country Club
Barnham Broom
Norwich, Norfolk,
England NR9 4DD
(44) 60545 393, Ext. 278
Fax: (44) 60545 8224

Year-round three- and
four-day schools in
Barnham Broom (February
to November) and
Portugal, Spain, and the
United States (November
to March)

There are approximately two million golfers under eighteen years of age in the United States alone. The PGA publishes its quarterly *Junior Golf Journal* to promote interest and participation in and enjoyment of golf by young people. This publication includes information on junior golf programs, instruction, health and fitness, equipment, minority golf, schedules and statistics, and much more. The PGA annually sponsors the PGA Junior Tournaments for girls and boys. For more information contact: The PGA Foundation, 100 Avenue of the Champions, Palm Beach Gardens, FL 33418. Tel: (407) 624-8400, Fax: (407) 624-7865.

The American Junior Golf Association, founded in 1977, now sponsors thirty-six events involving over 3,500 golfers ages thirteen through eighteen. Contact: American Junior Golf Association, 2415 SteeplechaseLane, Roswell, GA 30076, (404) 998-4653.

The United States Golf Association sponsors junior tournaments, including the Amateur Public Links, Junior Amateur, and Girls' Junior, and through its United States Golf foundation funds nonprofit junior golf programs, caddie programs, and assistance programs for the physically challenged. Contact: The United States Golf Foundation, P.O. Box 708, Far Hills, NJ 07931-0708, (908) 234-2300.

The Ladies Professional Golf Association offers junior girls' golf camps, inner-city golf programs, and a junior girls' golf club. Contact: LPGA, 2570 W. International Speedway Boulevard, Suite B, Daytona Beach, FL 32114, (909) 254-8800. For camp information contact: LPGA Junior Girls' Golf Camps, 12507 Kirkham Road, Louisville, KY 40299, (502) 244-8635.

Caddie program information can be obtained from state and local golf associations, including the Western Golf Association, 1 Briar Road, Golf, IL 60029, (609) 724-4600, which administers the Evans Scholar Foundation established by Charles "Chick" Evans in 1930. Evans, who caddied as a youth, won seven Western Amateurs (1909, 1912, 1914-15, 1920-23), two U.S. Amateurs (1916, 1920).

Also offering scholarship support to caddies are: The Francis Ouimet Caddie Scholarship Fund, named after the winner of the 1913 U.S. Open, 190 Park Road, Weston, MA 02193, (617) 891-6400; The William Riddy Neale Scholarship Fund, c/o Connecticut State Golf Association, 35 Cold Spring Road, No. 212, Rocky Hill, CT 06067, (203) 257-4171; and the Westchester Golf Association, 1875 Palmer Avenue, Room 204, Larchmont, NY 10538, (914) 834-5869.

A source of assistance for young people interested in golf at the collegiate level is the National Collegiate Athletic Association(NCAA), which provides *The NCAA Guide for the College-Bound Student-Athlete*, as well as other information. Contact: NCAA, Box 1906, Mission, KS 66201, (913) 384-3220. The National Association of Intercollegiate Athletics (NAIA) also conducts college golf programs and can be reached at NAIA, 1221 Baltimore, Kansas City, MO 64105, (816) 842-5050. A variety of publishers provide information on college athletic programs, entrance requirements and scholarship opportunities. *The American College Golf Guide* is available from Dean Frishknect Publishing, Box 1179, Hillsboro, OR 97123, (503) 648-1333. Peterson's Publishing offers a broad range of college guides: Peterson's Publishing, Box 2123, Princeton, NJ 08543-2123, (609) 243-9111, (800) 338-3282. And for a fee the College Golf Service provides assistance in searching for college golf scholarships and financial aid: College Golf Service, Box 2061, Danvers, MA 01923-5061, (508) 777-9828.

The National Golf Foundation is another source of support for young golfers. The foundation offers several publications on player development including *Golf Schools in the United States*, *Guide to U.S. Golf Scholarships*, *Start a Junior Golf Program: Build for the Future*, and others. National Golf Foundation, 1150 South U.S. Highway One, Suite 401, Jupiter, FL 33477, (407) 744-6006, (800) 733-6006.

Collingtree Park Golf Course/Academy
Windingbook Lane
Northampton, England
(44) 604 700000

One- to five-day schools held from March to September at Collingtree Park Golf Course

French-American Center Stay and Study Program
c/o Travel Exchange, Ltd.
1154 E. Putnam Avenue
Riverside, CT 06878
(203) 698-1900
(800) 248-0248
Fax: (203) 698-1080

Two two-week programs in August at Avignon's 18-hole Chateaublanc course

Peter Green Golf Camp
Village Camps
1296 Coppet
Switzerland
(41) 22 776 2059
Fax: (41) 22 776 2060

Camps for ten- to eighteen-year-olds. Three two-week camps fron mid-July to mid-August in Switzerland, France, England, Australia, and the United States

Jamaica Jamaica Golf School
c/o International Lifestyles
(516) 868-6924
(800) 858-8009
or
Jamaica Jamaica Hotel
P. O. Box 58
Runaway Bay
St. Ann, Jamaica, W.I.
(809) 973-2346

Year-round schools at the Runaway Bay Golf Course

John Jacobs' Practical Golf Schools
7825 E. Redfield Road
Scottsdale, AZ
85260-6977
(602) 991-8587
(800) 472-5007
Fax: (602) 991-8243

More than 800 two-to five-day schools year-round at a variety of U.S. locations and Indonesia, China, England, Austria, Germany, and Spain. Junior programs are held during the summer

Residential Golf Schools
Langley House
Langley Mill
Nottingham, England
NG16 4AN
(44) 773 530777/769864
Fax: (44) 773 530862

Offers more than 100 weekly two- to twelve-day schools year-round in Great Britain, France, Germany, Denmark, and Florida

Tryall Golf Schools
Tryall Golf, Tennis
and Beach Club
P. O. Box 1206
Montego Bay, Jamaica,
W. I.
(800) 742-0498

Three-day schools in March at the Tryall Golf Course

The first book entirely dedicated to golf, *The Goff: An Heroi-Comical Poem in Three Cantos*, is a 24-page extended poem written by Thomas Mathison and published in Scotland in 1743. Few golf collectibles of any kind dating before the nineteenth century can be found today. A copy of *The Goff* would fetch several thousand dollars if it appeared on the open market. Since *The Goff* was issued, thousands of golf books have been published on history, architecture, equipment, rules, travel, biography, humor, instruction, and esoteric aspects of the game such as *How to Build Your Own Putting Green*.

5

golf books and directories

The first substantial American golf book was *Golf in America*, written by James Lee and published in 1895. The first extensive effort at compiling a golf bibliography was *Collecting Golf Books*, written by Cecil Hopkinson in 1938. Other notable bibliographies include *The Library of Golf*, written by Joe Murdoch in 1968, and *Golf-A Guide to Information Sources*, developed by Joe Murdoch with Janet Seagle and published in 1979.

The number of golf books being published is on the rise, including reprints of classics such as Bernard Darwin's *The Darwin Sketchbook* (essays from

1910 to 1955); Alister Mackenzie's *Golf Architecture* (1920); Robert T. Jones, Jr., and O. B. Keeler's *Down the Fairway* (1927); Charles Blair Macdonald's *Scotland's Gift -Golf* (1928); Herbert Warren Wind's *The Story of American Golf* (1948); and Dan Jenkins' *The Dogged Victims of Inexorable Fate* (1970). Herbert Warren Wind and Robert S. Macdonald, through their superb "The Classics of Golf " book program, have made these volumes available at reasonable prices. Golf memorabilia and collectibles experts such as George and Susan Lewis at Golfiana in Mamaroneck, New York, can find you original copies and other volumes essential to your own golf book collection.

Among the more recent books that I have enjoyed are *The U.S. Open* by Robert Sommers (1987); *Golf's Golden Grind* by Al Barkow (1974); *The Anatomy of a Golf Course* by Tom Doak (1992); *The Architects of Golf* by Geoffrey Cornish and Ronald E. Whitten (revised, 1993); *The Illustrated History of Women's Golf* by Rhonda Glenn (1991); *The World Atlas of Golf* edited by Pat-Ward Thomas, Herbert Warren Wind, Charles Price, and Peter Thomson (revised, 1991); *Bury Me in a Pot Bunker* by Pete Dye (1994); *Golf Courses of the PGA Tour* by George Peper (second edition, 1994); *The Great Golf Courses of Canada* by John Gordon (1991); and *The Golfer's Home Companion* by Robin McMillan et. al. (1994). *Harvey Penick's Little Red Book* by Harvey Penick with Bud Shrake (1992) is the all-time best-selling golf book with several hundred thousand copies sold.

There are many good books and popular categories (such as instruction, humor, and collectibles) not covered in the above lists.

Each collector or reader of golf books obviously gravitates to his or her own interests. For the sake of brevity and practicality, below is a short list of recommended books for a basic golf library. If you need more assistance sorting through the morass of golf books now available, consult the United States Golf Association, a reputable dealer in golf books, or your local book store or library.

GOLF BOOKS

Instruction

Allen, Frank Kenyon; Tom LoPresti; Dale Mead; and Barbara Romack. *Golfer's Bible.* New York: Doubleday, 1968.

Allis, Percy. *Better Golf.* London: A. & C. Black, 1926.

Allis, Peter, and Paul Trevillion. *Easier Golf.* London: Stanley Paul. 1969.

Armour, Tommy. *How to Play Your Best Golf All the Time.* New York: Simon and Schuster. 1953.

Aultman, Dick, and Ken Bowden. *The Methods of Golf's Masters.* New York: Coward, McCann and Geoghegan, Inc., 1975.

Barber, Jerry. *The Art of Putting.* Los Angeles: LaLanne-Barber. 1967.

Ballesteros, Seve, with John Andrisani. *Natural Golf.* New York: Atheneum, 1988.

Barnes, James M. *Picture Analysis of Golf Strokes.* Philadelphia: J. B. Lippincott Co., 1919.

Baughman, Ernest A. *How to Caddie.* Chicago: Privately printed. 1914.

Bell, Peggy Kirk, and Jerry Clausen. *A Woman's Way to Better Golf.* New York: E. P. Dutton & Co., 1966.

Berg, Patty, and Otis Dypwick. *Golf.* New York: Alfred A. Knopf, 1946.

Blanchard, Ken. *Playing the Great Game of Golf: Making Every Minute Count.* Kentucky: Blanchard Family Partnership, 1992.

Boomer, Percy. *On Learning Golf.* New York: Alfred A. Knopf, 1946.

Boros, Julius. *How to Play Golf With an Effortless Swing.* Englewood Cliffs, NJ: Prentice-Hall, 1964.

Braid, James. *Advanced Golf, or Hints and Instruction for Progressive Players.* Philadelphia: George W. Jacobs, 1927.

—, and Harry Vardon. *How to Play Golf* (from the Spalding Athletic Library). New York: American Sports, 1928.

Brown, Robert. *The Golfing Mind.* New York: Lyons & Burford, 1994.

Casper, Billy. *Golf Shotmaking With Billy Casper.* Garden City, NY: Doubleday & Co., 1966.

Charles, Bob, with Roger P. Ganem. *Left-Handed Golf.* Englewood Cliffs, NJ: Prentice-Hall, 1965.

Cochran, Alastair, and John Stobbs. *Then Search for the Perfect Golf Swing.* London: Heinemann, 1968.

Cotton, Henry. *Study the Game With Henry Cotton.* London: Country Life, 1964.

Diegle, Leo, and Jim Dante with Len Elliot. *The Nine Bad Shots of Golf.* New York: Whittlesly House, 1947.

Dunn, Seymour. *Golf Fundamentals.* Trumbull, CT: Golf Digest Books, 1986.

East, Victor J. *Better Golf in 5 Minutes.* Englewood Cliffs, NJ: Prentice-Hall, 1956.

Farnie, Henry Brougham. The Golfer's Manual Being an Historical and Descriptive Account of the National Game of Scotland. Cupar: Whitehead and Orr, 1857

Flick, Jim, and Dick Aultman. *Square to Square: Golf in Pictures: An Illustrated History of the Modern Swing Techniques.* Nowalk, CT: Golf Digest. 1974.

Flick, Jim, and Bob Toski. *How to Become a Complete Golfer.* Norwalk, CT: Golf Digest Books, 1978.

Floyd, Raymond. *From 60 Yards In.* New York: Harper & Row, 1989.

Gallway, Timothy W. *The Inner Game of Golf.* New York: Random House, 1981.

Geiberger, Al, with Larry Dennis. *Tempo, Golf's Master Key: How to Find It, How to Keep It.* Norwalk, CT: Golf Digest Books, 1980.

Golf Digest [Editorial staff]. *Instant Golf Lessons.* Norwalk, CT: Golf Digest Books, 1978.

Golf Digest [Editorial staff]. *80 Five-Minute Golf Lessons.* Englewood Cliffs, NJ: Prentice-Hall, 1968.

Golf Magazine [Editorial staff]. *Golf Magazine's Handbook of Putting.* New York: Harper & Row, 1973.

Grout, Jack, with Dick Aultman. *Let Me Teach You Golf as I Taught Jack Nicklaus.* New York: Atheneum, 1975.

Haynie, Sandra. *Golf: A Natural Course for Women.* New York: Atheneum, 1975.

Hebron, Michael. *The Art and Zen of Learning Golf.* Smithtown, NY: Privately published, 1990.

Hilton, Harold. *Modern Golf.* New York: Outing, 1913.

Hogan, Ben, and Herbert Warren Wind. *Ben Hogan's Five Lessons — The Modern Fundamentals of Golf.* New York: A. S. Barnes, 1957.

Hutchinson, Horace G. *Hints on the Game of Golf.* Edinburgh and London: William Blackwood and Sons, 1886.

Jacobs, John. *The Golf Swing Simplified.* New York: Lyons & Burford, 1994.

Jacobs, John. *Practical Golf.* New York: Quadrangle, 1972.

Kite, Tom, with Larry Dennis. *How To Play Consistent Golf.* Trumbull, CT: Golf Digest Books, 1990.

Jobe, Frank W., M.D., with Diane R. Moynes. *Thirty Exercises for Better Golf.* Inglewood, CA: Champion Press, 1989.

Jones, Ernest, and Innis Brown. *Swinging Into Golf.* New York: McGraw-Hill, 1937.

Jones, Ernest, and David Eisenberg. *Swing the Club-head.* New York: Dodd Mead, 1952.

Jones, Robert Tyre, Jr. *Bobby Jones on Golf.* New York: Doubleday, 1966.

Leadbetter, David. *David Leadbetter's Faults and Fixes.* New York: HarperCollins, 1993.

Leadbetter, David. *The Golf Swing.* New York: Viking Penguin Books, 1990.

Low, John L. *Concerning Golf.* London: Hodder & Stoughton, 1903.

Low, George, with Al Barkow. *The Master of Putting.* New York: Atheneum, 1986.

MacDonald, Bob. *Golf.* Chicago: Wallace Press, 1927.

Massy, Arnaud. *Golf.* New York: Brentanos, 1922.

McCarthy, Colman. *The Pleasures of the Game.* New York: Dial Press, 1977.

McLean, Jim. *The Eight-Step Golf Swing: A Revolu-tionary Golf Technique by a Pro Coach.* New York: HarperCollins, 1994.

McLean, Jim, with Larry Dennis. *Golf Digest's Book Of Drills.* Trumbull, CT: Golf Digest Books, 1990.

Middlecoff, Cary. *Cary Middlecoff's Master Guide to Golf.* Englewood Cliffs, NJ: Prentice-Hall, 1960.

—*The Golf Swing.* Engle-wood Cliffs, NJ: Prentice-Hall, 1974.

Miller, Johnny, with Dale Shankland. *Pure Golf.* New York: Doubleday, 1976.

Morrison, Alex J. *A New Way to Better Golf.* New York: Simon & Schuster, 1932.

National Golf Founda-tion. *Twelve Comprehensive, Professional Golf Lessons.* Revised edition. Jupiter, FL: The National Golf Foundation, 1985.

Nelson, Byron, with Larry Dennis. *Shape Your Swing the Modern Way.* Norwalk, CT: Golf Digest Books, 1976.

Nicklaus, Jack, with Ken Bowden. *Golf My Way.* New York: Simon & Schuster, 1974.

—*Jack Nicklaus's Lesson Tee.* Norwalk CT: Golf Digest Books, 1977.

—*Play Better Golf: The Swing From A to Z.* New York: Simon & Schuster, 1980.

Park, Willie Jr. *The Game of Golf.* London: Long-mans, Green, and Com-pany, 1896.

Penick, Harvey, with Bud Shrake. *Harvey Penick's Lit-tle Red Book: Lessons and Teachings from a Lifetime in Golf.* New York: Simon & Schuster, 1992.

Peper, George. *Scrambling Golf: How to Get Out of Trouble and into the Cup.* Englewood Cliffs, NJ: Prentice-Hall, 1977.

Professional Golf Association of America. *PGA Teaching Manual: The Art and Science of Golf Instruction.* Palm Beach Gardens, FL: PGA, 1990.

Player, Gary. *Fit For Golf: One Hundred Exercises That Will Improve Your Game— Whatever Your Age, Whatever Your Handicap.* New York: Simon & Schuster, 1995.

—, with Desmond Tolhurst. *Golf Begins At 50.* New York: Simon & Schuster, 1988.

Runyan, Paul. *Paul Runyan's Book for Senior Golfers.* New York: Dodd, Mead, 1962.

—, with Dick Aultman. *The Short Way to Lower Scoring.* Norwalk, CT: Golf Digest Books, 1979.

Saunders, Vivien. *The Golfing Mind.* London: Stanley Paul & Co., 1984.

Simpson, Sir Walter G. *The Art of Golf.* Edinburgh: Dave Douglas, 1887.

Smith, Alex. *Lessons in Golf.* New York: Grannis Press, 1904.

Smith, Horton, and Dawson Taylor. *The Secret of . . . Holing Putts.* New York: A. S. Barnes, 1961.

Snead, Sam. *How to Hit a Golf Ball.* New York: Doubleday, 1950.

Suggs, Louise. *Par Golf for Women.* New York: Prentice-Hall, 1953.

Travers, J. D. *Travers' Golf Book.* New York: Macmillan, 1913.

Travis, Walter. *Practical Golf.* New York: Harper and Brothers, 1901.

Vardon, Harry. *The Complete Golfer.* New York: McLure Phillips, 1905.

—*The Gist of Golf.* New York: Doran, 1922.

Venturi, Ken, with Al Barkow. *The Venturi Analysis: Learning Golf from the Champions.* New York: Atheneum, 1981.

Watson, Tom, with Nick Seitz. *Getting Up and Down: How to Save Strokes from Forty Yards and In.* New York: Random House, 1983.

Whitworth, Kathy, with Rhonda Glenn. *Golf for Women.* New York: St. Martin's Press, 1990.

Wind, Herbert Warren. *Tips from the Top.* New York: Prentice-Hall, 1955.

Wiren, Gary. *The PGA Manual of Golf: The Professional's Way to Play Better Golf.* New York: MacMillan, 1991.

Wright, Mickey. *Play Golf the Wright Way.* New York: Doubleday & Company, 1962.

Zaharias, Mildred "Babe." *Championship Golf.* New York: A. S. Barnes, 1948.

Women in Golf

Barton, Pam. *A Stroke a Hole.* London: Blackie, 1937.

Collett (Vare), Glenna. *Ladie in the Rough.* New York: Alfred A. Knopf, 1928.

Cossey, Rosalynde. *Golfing Ladies.* London: Orbis, 1984.

Glenn, Rhonda. *The Illustrated History of Women's Golf.* Dallas, TX: Taylor Publishing, 1991.

Helme, Eleanor E. *After the Ball.* London: Hurst & Blackett, 1930.

Helme, Eleanor E., ed. *The Best of Golf: From Some of the Best Golfers.* London: Mills and Boon, 1925.

Kennard, Mrs. Edward. *The Sorrows of a Golfer's Wife.* London: F.V. White 1896.

Koch, Margaret. *The Pasatiempo Story.* Santa Cruz, CA: Pasatiempo Golf Club, 1990.

Leitch, Cecil. *Golf.* Philadelphia: Lippincott, 1922.

—*Golf Simplified.* London: Thornton Butlerworth, 1924.

Lopez, Nancy, with Peter Schwed. *Education of a Woman Golfer.* 1979.

Macdonald, Robert S., and Herbert Warren Wind, eds. *The Great Women Golfers.* New York: Ailsa, 1994.

Robertson, Belle, and Lewine Mair. *The Woman Golfer: A Lifetime of Golfing Success.* Edinburgh: Mainstream, 1988.

Robertson, Maud Gordon. *Hints to Lady Golfers.* London: Walbrook, 1909.

Saunders, Vivien. *The Complete Woman Golfer.* London: Stanley Paul, 1986.

Wethered, Joyce. *Golfing Memories and Methods.* London: Hutchinson and Co., 1933.

Wilson, Enid. *A Gallery of Women Golfers.* London: Country Life, 1961.

—Golf for Women. London: Arthur Baker, 1964.

Zaharias, Mildred "Babe." *This Life I've Led.* New York: A. S. Barnes, 1955.

Junior Golf

Bryan, Dorothy and Marguerite. *Michael & Patsy on the Golf Links.* Garden City, NY: Doubleday, Doran, 1933.

Collett, Glenna. *Golf for Young Players.* Boston: Little Brown, 1926.

Cotton, Henry. *Golf: Being a Short Treatise for the Use of Young People who Aspire to Proficiency in the Royal and Ancient Game.* London: Eyre & Spottiswode, 1939.

Evans, Chick. *Chick Evans' Golf for Boys and Girls.* Chicago and New York: Windsor Press, 1954.

Ford, Doug. *Start Golf Young.* New York: Sterling, 1955.

Golf Digest [Editorial staff]. *Better Golf for Boys.* New York: Dodd Mead, 1965.

Golf Digest [Editorial staff]. *A Golden Pocket Guide: Golf.* New York: Golden Press, 1968.

Hayes, Larry, with Rhonda Glenn. *The Junior Golf Book: An Instructional for Beginning Players, Ages 8-18.* New York: St. Martins Press, 1994.

Krause, Peter. *Fundamental Golf.* Minneapolis: Lerner, 1994.

Leitch, Cecil. *Golf for Girls.* New York: American Sports Publishing Co., 1912.

Miller, Johnny, with Desmond Tolhurst. *Johnny Miller's Golf for Juniors: Basic Principles of the Game.* New York: Doubleday, 1987.

Ouimet, Francis. *Golf Facts for Young People.* New York: Century, 1921.

U.S. Junior Chamber of Commerce. *Jaycee Junior Golf: Instructional Handbook.* U.S. Junior Chamber of Commerce, 1962.

Wiren, Gary. *Planning and Conducting a Junior Golf Program.* Chicago: The National Golf Foundation, 1973.

Golf History

Allis, Peter, with Michael Hobbs. *The Open: The British Open Golf Championship Since the War.* London: Collins, 1984.

Barkow, Al. *Gettin' to the Dance Floor.* New York: Atheneum, 1986.

—Golf's Golden Grind. New York and London: Harcourt Brace Jovanovich, 1974.

Barclay, James. *Golf in Canada.* Canada: McClelland & Stewart Inc., 1992.

Bisher, Furman. *The Masters: Augusta Revisted.* Birmingham, AL: Oxmoor, 1976.

Browning, Robert. *A History of Golf: The Royal and Ancient Game.* London: J.M. Dent & Sons, 1955.

Clark, Robert. *Golf: A Royal and Ancient Game.* Second edition. London: Macmillan & Co., 1893.

Colville, George M. *Five Open Champions and the Musselburgh Golf Story.* Musselburgh: Privately Published, 1890.

Darwin, Bernard. *Golf Between the Two Wars.* London: Chatto & Windus, 1944.

—, et al. *A History of Golf in Britain.* London: Cassells, 1952.

Dobereiner, Peter. *The Glorious World of Golf.* New York: McGraw-Hill, 1973.

Everard, H.S.C. *A History of the Royal and Ancient Golf Club: St. Andrews, From 1754 to 1900.* Edinburgh: Blackwood, 1907.

Gibson, William H. *Early Irish Golf.* Naas: Oakleaf Publications, 1988.

Graffis, Herb. *The PGA: The Official History of the Professional Golfer's Association of America.* New York: T. Y. Crowell, 1975.

Henderson, Ian, and David Stirk. *Golf in the Making.* Crawley, England: Henderson & Stirk, 1979.

Hutchinson, Horace. *Fifty Years of Golf.* London: Constable, 1919.

Kavanagh, L. V. *History of Golf in Canada.* Toronto: Fitzhenry and Whiteside, 1973.

Lee, James P. *Golf in America: A Practical Manual.* New York: Dodd, Mead, 1895.

Lema, Tony. *Golfer's Gold: An Inside View of the Pro Tour.* Boston: Little, Brown & Co., 1964.

MacDonald, Charles Blair. *Scotland's Gift: Golf.* New York: Charles Scribner's Sons, 1928.

Martin, H. B. *Fifty Years of American Golf.* New York: Dodd, Mead, 1936.

Mathison, Thomas. *The Goff: An Heroi-Comical Poem in Three Cantos.* Edinburgh, Scotland: Privately published, 1743.

Pace, Lee. *Pinehurst Stories.* Pinehurst, NC: Resorts of Pinehurst, 1991.

Peper, George; Robin McMillan; and James A. Frank. Golf in America: The First 100 *Years.* New York: Harry Abrams, 1988.

Price, Charles. *A Golf Story: Bobby Jones, Augusta National and the Masters Tournament.* New York: Atheneum, 1986.

—*The World of Golf: A Panorama of Six Centuries of the Game's History.* New York: Random House, 1962.

Sommers, Robert. *The U.S. Open: Golf's Ultimate Challenge.* New York: Atheneum, 1987.

Van Hengel, Steven J.H. *Early Golf.* Amsterdam: Privately published, 1982.

Wind, Herbert Warren. *The Story of American Golf.* New York: Farrar, Strauss, 1948, 1956, 1975, 1986.

Biographies and Personal Accounts

Adamson, Alistair B. *Allan Robertson, Golfer: His Life and Times.* Worcestershire: Grant Books, 1985.

Allis, Peter. *Peter Allis: An Autobiography.* London: Collins, 1981.

Boswell, Charlie, with Curt Anders. *Now I See.* New York: Merideth, 1969.

Corcoran, Fred. *Unplayable Lies.* New York: Duell, Sloan and Pearce, 1965.

Darwin, Bernard. *James Braid.* London: Hodder & Stoughton, 1952.

Demaret, Jimmy. *My Partner, Ben Hogan.* New York: McGraw-Hill, 1954.

Evans, Charles "Chick." *Chick Evans' Golf Book.* New York, San Francisco, and Chicago: Thomas E. Wilson, 1969.

Howell, Audrey. *Harry Vardon: The Revealing Story of a Champion Golfer.* London: Stanley Paul, 1991.

Hagen, Walter, with Margaret Seaton Heck. *The Walter Hagen Story.* New York: Simon & Schuster, 1956.

Hauser, Thomas. *Arnold Palmer: A Personal Journey.* New York: HarperCollins, 1994.

Hilton, Harold H. *My Golfing Remembrances.* London: James Nisbet, 1907.

Jones, Robert T., Jr. *Golf is My Game.* Garden City, NY: Doubleday, 1960.

—and O. B. Keeler. *Down the Fairway.* New York: Minton, Balch and Company, 1927.

Kirkaldy, Andra, with Clyde Foster. *My Fifty Years of Golf: Memories.* London: T. Fisher Unwin, 1921.

Littler, Gene. *The Real Score.* Waco: Word Books, 1976.

Locke, Bobby. *Bobby Locke on Golf.* London: Country Life, 1953.

Longhurst, Henry. *My Life and Soft Times.* London: Cassell, 1971.

Low, John L. *F. G. Tait: A Record.* London: Nisbet and Co., 1900.

Melhorn, Bill, with Bobby Shave. *Golf Secrets Exposed.* Miami: M & S, 1984.

Nicklaus, Jack, with Herbert Warren Wind. *The Greatest Game of All: My Life in Golf.* New York: Simon & Schuster, 1969.

Ouimet, Frances. *A Game of Golf: A Book of Reminiscences.* Boston: Houghton Mifflin, 1932.

Palmer, Arnold. *Go for Broke.* New York: Simon & Schuster, 1973.

Plimpton, George. *The Bogey Man: A Month on the PGA Tour.* New York: Harper & Row, 1968; Lyons & Burford, 1993.

Sarazen, Gene. *Thirty Years of Championship Golf.* New York: Prentice-Hall, 1950.

Sanders, Doug, with Larry Sheehan. *Come Swing With Me: My Life On and Off the Tour.* Garden City, NY: Doubleday & Co., 1974.

Sifford, Charlie, with James Gallo. *Just Let Me Play: The Story of Charlie Sifford.* Latham: British American, 1992.

Snead, Sam. *The Education of a Golfer.* New York: Simon & Schuster, 1962.

Travers, Jerome G., and Grantland Rice. *The Winning Shot.* Garden City, NY: Doubleday, Page, 1915.

Trevino, Lee, and Sam Blair. *The Snake in the Sandtrap and Other Misadventures on the Golf Tour.* New York: Henry Holt, 1985.

Tulloch, W.W. *The Life of Tom Morris, With Glimpses of St. Andrews and its Golfing Celebrities.* London: T. Werner Laurie, 1908.

Vardon, Harry. *My Golfing Life.* London: Hutchinson, 1933.

Architecture and Golf Courses

Allen, Peter. *Play the Best Courses: Great Golf in the British Isles.* London: Stanley Paul, 1973.

Balfour, James. *Reminiscences of Golf on St. Andrews Links.* Edinburgh: David Douglas, 1887.

Colt, H. S. and C. H. Alison. *Some Essays on Golf Course Architecture.* New York: Charles Scribners and Sons, 1920.

Cornish, Geoffrey S., and William G. Robinson. *Golf Course Design: An Introduction.* Amherst, MA: Privately published, 1979.

Cornish, Geoffrey S., and Ronald E. Whitten. *The Golf Course.* New York: The Rutledge Press, 1981.

—*The Architects of Golf.* (A revised edition of *The Golf Course*). New York: HarperCollins, 1993.

Darwin, Bernard. *The Golf Courses of the British Isles.* London: Duckworth, 1910.

Dickinson, Patric. *A Round of Golf Course: A Selection of the Best Eighteen.* London: Evans Brothers, 1951.

Doak, Tom. *The Anatomy of a Golf Course: The Art of Golf Architecture.* New York: Lyons & Burford, 1992.

—*The Confidential Guide to Golf Courses.* Traverse City, MI: Renaissance Golf Design, Inc., 1994.

Dobereiner, Peter, with Gordon Richardson. *Golf Courses of the PGA European Tour.* London: Aurum Press, 1992.

Dye, Pete. *Bury Me in a Pot Bunker: Golf through the Eyes of the Game's Most Challenging Course Designer.* Reading, MA: Addison Wesley, 1995.

Europcar. *Golf Guide Europe.* Suresnes, France: Europcar, 1991.

Golf Digest [Editorial staff]. *A Paradise Called Pebble Beach.* Trumbull, CT: Golf Digest Books, 1992.

Gordon, John. *The Great Golf Courses of Canada.* Montreal and Toronto: McGraw-Hill, 1991.

Grant, Donald. *Donald Ross of Pinehurst and Royal Dornoch.* Golspie, Scotland: The Sutherland Press, 1973.

Hawtree, Fred. *Colt & Co.* Woodstock, Oxford: Cambuc Archive, 1991.

Hawtree, Fred. *The Golf Course: Planning, Design, Construction & Maintenance.* London: E. & F. N. Spon, 1983.

Hunter, Robert. *The Links.* New York: Charles Scribner's Sons, 1926.

Jenkins, Dan. *Sports Illustrated's The Best 18 Holes in America.* New York: Delacourte, 1966.

Jones, Robert Trent, Jr. *Golf By Design: How To Lower Your Score by Reading the Features of a Course.* Boston and New York: Little, Brown and Co., 1993.

Labbance, Bob, and David Cornwell. *The Golf Courses of New Hampshire: From the Mountains to the Sea.* Stockbridge, VT: New England Golf Specialists, 1989.

—*The Maine Golf Guide.* Stockbridge, VT: New England Golf Specialists, 1991.

—*Vermont Golf Courses: A Player's Guide.* Shelburne, VT: New England Press, 1987.

Mackenzie, Alister. *Golf Architecture.* London: Simpkin, Marshall, Hamilton & Kent, 1920.

— The Secret of St. Andrews. Chelsea, MI: Sleeping Bear Press, 1995.

Martin, J. Peter. *Adirondack Golf Courses: Past And Present.* Lake Placid, NY: Adirondack Golf, 1987.

McCallen, Brian. *Golf Resorts of the World: The Best Places to Stay and Play.* New York: Harry Abrams, 1993.

McCord, Robert. *The 479 Best Public Golf Courses in the United States, Canada, the Caribbean and Mexico.* New York: Random House, 1993.

National Golf Course Directory, Volume II. Springfield, MO: National Golf Course Directory Publishing, 1994.

Peper, George. *Golf Courses of the PGA Tour.* New York: Harry N. Abrams, 1986; revised edition 1994.

Price, Robert. *Scotland's Golf Courses.* Aberdeen, Scotland: Aberdeen University Press, 1989.

Springman, J.F. *The Beauty of Pebble Beach.* Philadelphia: Baum, 1964.

Steel, Donald. *Classic Golf Links of Great Britain and Ireland.* London: Edburg & Pelham, 1975.

Strawn, John. *Driving the Green: The Making of a Golf Course.* New York: HarperCollins, 1991.

Thomas, George C. *Golf Course Architecture in America: Its Strategy and Construction.* Los Angeles: Times Mirror Press, 1927.

Ward-Thomas, Pat. *The Royal and Ancient.* Edinburgh: Scottish Academy Press, 1980.

—Herbert Warren Wind, Charles Price, Peter Thomson, and Donald Steel. *The World Atlas of Golf.* London: Mitchell Beazley Publishers, 1976; revised editions 1988, 1991.

Wethered, H. N. and T. Simpson. *The Architectural Side of Golf.* London: Longman's Green, 1929.

Rules and Etiquette

Chapman, Hay. *The Law of the Links: Rules, Principles and Etiquette of Golf.* San Francisco: Privately printed, 1922.

Clapcott, C. B. *The History of Handicapping.* Privately printed, 1924.

Cromie, Charles. *Rules of Golf Illustrated.* London: Golf Illustrated, 1905.

Cousins, Geoffrey. *Golfers at Law.* New York: Knopf, 1959.

Eberl, George. *Golf is a Good Walk Spoiled.* Dallas, TX: Taylor Publishing, 1993.

Gould, David. *Do It Right: A Guide to a Proper and Civilized Golf Game.* New York: Fairchild Publications, 1994.

United States Golf Association. *Decisions on the Rules of Golf.* Far Hills, NJ: USGA, updated periodically.

Watson, Tom, with Frank Hannigan. *The Rules of Golf Illustrated and Explained.* New York: Random House, 1980; Revised edition, 1992.

Equipment

Abrahams, Jonathan. *Golf Smarts: Buying Golf Clubs That Work.* New York: Lyons & Burford, 1994.

Hogan, Bill. *Golf Gadgets: The Ultimate Catalog of Golf Equipment and Accessories.* New York: Macmillan, 1989.

Maltby, Ralph D. *Golf Club Design, Fitting, Alteration and Repair.* Newark, OH: Faultless Sports, 1974; Revised edition, Newark, OH: Ralph Maltby Enterprises, 1982.

Paul, Carl. *Golf Clubmaking and Repair.* Austin, TX: Paul Assoc., 1984.

References

Bauchope, C. Robertson, John Bauchope, and David Scott Duncan. *Golfing Annual.* London: Horace Cox, 1888-1910.

Chattell, C. C. *Golfers' Guide 1908: A Complete Handbook of Useful Information for Golf Clubs and Their Members.* Chicago: Lakeside Press, 1908 and 1909.

Cox, Leo D. *Fraser's International Golf Year Book.* Montreal and New York: Fraser Publishing Co., 1923-1937.

Cox, Charles S., Thomas Bendelow, Charles Kirchner, and Grantland Rice. *Spalding's Official Golf Guide.* New York: American Sports Publishing Co., 1897-1932.

Davies, Peter. *Davies Dictionary of Golfing Terms.* New York: Simon & Schuster, 1980.

Gibson, Nevin H. *The Encyclopedia of Golf.* New York: A. S. Barnes & Co., 1958.

Golf Magazine [Editorial staff]. *Golf Magazine's Encyclopedia of Golf.* New York: Harper Collins, 1993.

Honorable Secretary, ed. *Ladies Golf Union Annual* (now titled *The Ladies Golf Union Yearbook*). England: Various places and publishers, since 1894 (except during World War I and II).

Low, John L., and Vyvyan G. Harnesworth, eds. *Nisbet's Golf Year Book.* London: James Nisbet, 1905-1914.

Mathieson, Donald M.; R. D. Mathieson; and William C. Goldie, eds. *Golfer's Handbook.* Edinburgh and Glasgow: 1898-1941 and 1946 to present.

McCormack, Mark. *World of Professional Golf.* (Issued under various titles.) Various places and publishers 1967 to present. Currently published in Cleveland, OH: International Management Group.

McMillan, Robin, et al. *The Golfer's Home Companion.* New York: Simon & Schuster, 1993.

Ladies Professional Golf Association. *LPGA Player Guide.* Daytona Beach, FL: LPGA, annually since 1950.

If you asked avid golfers, all could cite their favorite courses or the one course that they would play if they only had one last round on this planet. The list would undoubtedly be long. But most of us have limited time and resources. So here is a short list of courses you must play before reaching that Big Clubhouse in the Sky.

1. ST. ANDREWS, Old Course, St. Andrews, Scotland. The birthplace of golf and site of many British Opens and other significant championships. Links golf at its quirky best.

2. AUGUSTA NATIONAL, Augusta, Georgia, U.S.A. Home of the Masters and the legend of Bobby Jones, codesigner of the course with Alister Mackenzie.

3. PEBBLE BEACH, Pebble Beach, California, U.S.A. A classic seaside golf course and site of many exciting tournaments including the epic Watson and Nicklaus duel in the 1982 U.S. Open. Nearby courses such as Cypress Point, Spanish Bay, and Spyglass Hill don't have the same tradition.

4. PINEHURST NO. 2, Pinehurst, North Carolina, U.S.A. This Donald Ross parkland course with its majestic white-verandaed clubhouse and "Maniac Hill" practice area has hosted the North and South Open, a major event in the old days, and will host the U.S. Open in 1999.

5. PINE VALLEY, Clementon, New Jersey, U.S.A. A throwback to the days of penal and very private boys-only golf, Pine Valley, designed by George Crump and H. S. Colt, has long been rated one of the best and most difficult courses in the world.

6. SHINNECOCK HILLS, Southampton, New York, U.S.A. Most recently the site of Corey Pavin's gritty victory in the 1995 U.S. Open, Shinnecock was one of the original five clubs that formed the United States Golf Association.

7. OAKMONT, Oakmont, Pennsylvania, U.S.A. Originally designed by William and Henry Fownes in 1903, Oakmont is another example of a great golf course created by amateur architects who had an excellent feel for the game and terrain.

8. WINGED FOOT, West Course, Mamaroneck, New York, U.S.A. A. W. Tillinghast, who also designed Baltusrol, Bethpage Black, San Francisco, and other great courses, artfully wove this course through an arboretum setting north of New York City. The old-style tricky contoured greens and high-faced bunkers present considerable difficulty on this golf layout.

9. BALLYBUNION, Old Course, County Kerry, Ireland. The dunes and ridges of sandhills perpendicular to the ocean bordering this course make it a windswept challenge on the west coast of Ireland. This classic linksland course, which Robert Trent Jones called "perhaps the finest piece of linksland in the world," has hosted many Irish championships.

10. ROYAL DORNOCH, Sutherland, Scotland. Situated six hundred miles to the north of London, Royal Dornoch is on the same latitude as the Bering Sea and Hudson Bay. A natural linksland course with seaside turf, dunes, hummocks, and other natural subtleties, including winds from the nearby sea, valleys, and mountains, Royal Dornoch is worth the pilgrimage.

Murdoch, Joseph. *Library of Golf 1743-1966.* Detroit: Gale Research Co., 1968. Addendum privately published in 1978.

—and Janet Seagle. *Golf— A Guide to Information Sources.* Detroit: Gale Research, 1979.

Professional Golf Association of America. *Official Media Guide of the PGA Tour.* Ponte Vedra, FL: PGA Tour, annually since 1941.

—*Official Media Guide of the Senior PGA Tour.* Ponte Vedra, FL: PGA Tour, annually since 1980.

Steel, Donald, Peter Ryde, and Herbert Warren Wind, eds. New York: The Viking Press, 1975.

United States Golf Association. *Record Book of U.S.G.A. Championships and International Events.* 2 vols. Far Hills, NJ: USGA, 1895-1959, and 1960-1980. Media guides annually thereafter.

Western Golf Association. *Caddie Operations Manual.* Golf, IL: Western Golf Association, 1969.

Golf Collections and Anthologies

Bartlett, Michael. *The Golf Book.* New York: Arbor House, 1980.

Darwin, Bernard, H. Gardner-Hill, Sir Guy Campbell, and others (contributors). *A History of Golf in Britain.* London: Cassell, 1952.

Dobereiner, Peter, ed. *Down the Nineteenth Fairway.* New York: Atheneum, 1983.

Hilton, Harold, and Garden C. Smith, eds. *The Royal and Ancient Game of Golf.* London: For *Golf Illustrated* by the London and Counties Press Association, 1912.

Hutchinson, Horace. Edited by the Duke of Beaufort. *Golf* (The Badminton Library.) London: Longmans, Green & Company, 1890.

Morrison, Alec, ed. *The Impossible Art of Golf: An Anthology of Golf Writing.* London and New York: Oxford University Press, 1995.

Price, Charles, ed. *The American Golfer.* New York: Random House, 1954.

Sports Illustrated [Editorial staff] *Golf: Four Decades of Sports Illustrated's Finest Writing on the Game of Golf.* Birmingham, AL: Oxmoor House, 1994.

Whethered, Roger and Joyce. *The Game of Golf* (Volume IX, The Lonsdale Library). London: Seeley, Service, 1931.

Wilson, Mark, and Ken Bowden, eds. *The Best of Henry Longhurst.* New York: Simon & Schuster, 1978.

Wodehouse, P.G. *The Golf Omnibus.* London: Barrie & Jenkins, 1973.

Wind, Herbert Warren, ed. *The Complete Golfer.* New York: Simon & Schuster, 1954.

Golf Essays

Bamberger, Michael. *To The Linksland: A Golfing Adventure.* New York: Penguin Books U.S.A., 1992.

Bantock, Miles. *On Many Greens: A Book of Golf and Golfers.* New York: Grosset & Dunlap, 1901.

Boswell, Thomas. *Strokes of Genius.* Garden City, NY: Doubleday & Co., 1987.

Darwin, Bernard. *A Friendly Round.* London: Stanley Paul, 1981.

Dobereiner, Peter. *For the Love of Golf—The Best of Dobereiner.* London: Stanley Paul, 1981.

Haultain, Arnold. *The Mystery of Golf.* Boston and New York: Houghton Mifflin, 1908.

Hay, Alex. *The Handbook of Golf.* London: Pelham, 1984.

Jenkins, Dan. *The Dogged Victims of Inexorable Fate.* Boston and Toronto: Little, Brown & Co., 1970.

Leach, Henry. *The Spirit of the Links.* London: Methuen, 1907.

Longhurst, Henry. *Talking About Golf.* London: MacDonald, 1966.

Price, Charles. *Golfer-At-Large.* New York: Atheneum, 1982.

Rice, Grantland. *The Duffer's Handbook of Golf.* New York: Macmillan, 1926.

Ryde, Peter, ed. *Mostly Golf: A Bernard Darwin Anthology.* London: A. & C. Black, 1976.

Simpson, Sir Walter G. *The Art of Golf.* Edinburgh: David Douglas, 1887.

Spander, Art, and Mark Mulvoy. *Golf, the Passion and the Challenge.* New York: Rutledge Books, 1977.

Stewart, Thomas P., ed. *A Tribute to Golf.* Harbor Springs, MI: Stewart, Hunter & Assoc., 1995.

Wade, Don. *And Then Jack Said To Arne . . .* Chicago: Contemporary Books, 1993.

Wind, Herbert Warren. *Following Through.* New York: Ticknor & Fields, 1985.

Wind, Herbert Warren. *Herbert Warren Wind's Golf Book.* New York: Simon & Schuster, 1971.

Golf Fiction

Adams, Herbert. *The Body in the Bunker.* New York: Lippincott, 1935.

Allerton, Mark. *The Girl on the Green.* London: Methuen, 1914.

Allis, Peter. *The Duke.* London: New English Library, 1983.

Anderson, Robert. *A Funny Thing Happened on the Way to the Clubhouse.* London: Arthur Barker, 1971.

Baert, Raymond. *The Adventures of Monsieur DuPont, Golf Champion.* London: Laurence & Jellicoe, 1913.

Ball, Brian. *Death of a Low Handicap Man.* New York: Walker, 1974.

Banes, Ford. *Right Down Your Fairway.* New York: A. S. Barnes, 1947.

Barker, Reg. *Eighteen is Forever.* Pretoria, South Africa: Privately published, 1959.

Brown, Horace. *Murder in the Rough.* London: T. V. Boardman, 1948.

Brown, Kenneth. *Putter Perkins.* Boston: Houghton Mifflin, 1923.

Bruff, Nancy. *The Country Club.* New York: Bartholomew House, 1969.

Christie, Agatha. *Murder on the Links.* London: John Lane, 1923.

Compston, Archie, and Stanley Anderson. *Love on the Fairway: A Romance of the Open Championship.* London: T. Werner Laurie, 1936.

Frome, David. *Murder on the Sixth Hole.* London: Methuen & Co., 1931.

Gault, William Campbell. *The Long Green.* New York: E. P. Dutton & Co., 1965.

Hallberg, William. *The Rub of the Green.* New York: Doubleday & Co., 1988.

—, ed. *Perfect Lies: A Century of Great Golf Stories.* Garden City, NY: Doubleday & Co., 1989.

THE CLASSICS OF GOLF

"The Classics of Golf" is a golf book program developed by Robert MacDonald and Herbert Warren Wind. Mr. MacDonald and Mr. Wind have selected golf classics such as *Down the Fairway* by Robert T. Jones, Jr., and O.B. Keeler; *Scotland's Gift—Golf* by Charles B. Macdonald; *The Story of American Golf* by Herbert Warren Wind; *The Mystery of Golf* by Bernard Haultain, and other classics. The Classics of Golf series includes over thirty books hadsomely reprinted and rebound with editorial comment by Mr. Wind and others. The essays by Herbert Warren Wind are alone worth the price of the books, usually around twenty-five to thirty dollars. Contact: The Classics of Golf, 65 Commerce Road, Stamford, CT 06902.

Hall, Holworthy. *Dormie One and Other Golf Stories.* New York: The Century Club, 1917.

Marshall, Robert. *The Haunted Major (The Enchanted Golf Clubs).* New York: Stokes, 1920.

Murphy, Michael. *Golf in the Kingdom.* New York: The Viking Press, 1972.

Shaw, Joseph T. *Out of the Rough.* New York: Windward House, 1934.

Steele, Chester K. *The Golf Course Mystery.* Cleveland, OH: International Fiction Library, 1919.

Sutphen, W.G. Van T. *The Golficide and Other Tales of the Fair Green.* New York: Harper, 1898.

Wind, Herbert Warren. *On Tour With Harry Sprague.* New York: Simon & Schuster, 1960.

Wodehouse, P.G. *Fore!: The Best of Wodehouse on Golf.* New York and New Haven: Ticknor & Fields, 1983.

Wynne, Anthony. *Death of a Golfer.* Philadelphia: Lippincott, 1937.

Miscellany

Ferguson, Marvin H., ed. *Building Golf Holes for Good Turf Management.* New York: United States Golf Association, 1968.

National Golf Foundation. *Guidelines for Financing a Golf Course.* Jupiter, FL: National Golf Foundation, 1995

—*Planning and Conducting Competitive Events.* Jupiter, FL: National Golf Foundation, 1994

Oakley, R. A., and C. V. Piper. *Turf for Golf Courses.* New York: Macmillan, 1917.

6

golf periodicals

The first periodical devoted entirely to golf was appropriately called *Golf*, a weekly magazine first published in 1890, featuring announcements of forthcoming events, tournament results, golf course information, equipment innovations, and other useful information. In 1894, *The Golfer*, the first American golf magazine was published in New York. After World War I, the number of golf periodicals began to ascend along with the rising popularity of golf. Publications included *Canadian Golfer*, published from mid-1915 to 1936; and *American Golfer*, originally edited by Walter Travis, was published from November 1908 to January 1936. Many other publications including *10,000 Lakes Golf and Outdoor Magazine* (circa June 1927 to March 1928) and *Golfing Gentlewomen* (1913 to May 1916), were shorter lived.

Today's major American national golf publications include *Golf* magazine, which was founded in 1959 and *Golf Digest*, established in 1950 under the name *Arrowhead Golf Digest*.

The leading association publication is *Golf Journal*, published by the United States Golf Association since 1948. A medley of other national and regional magazines including *Golf For Women*, *Metropolitan Golfer*, *Senior Golfer*, *Golf Tips*, *Petersen's Golfing*, *Golf Illustrated*, *Executive Golfer*, and many others now dot the landscape. *GolfWeek*, the only golf weekly in the United States, covers the major tour events, the golf business, golf-course development, and news items of interest to golfers.

   Score magazine, established in 1981, is the leading Canadian golf publication; and the foremost British periodicals include *Golf Monthly, Golf World, Today's Golfer*, and *Golf Illustrated Weekly*. In addition to national, regional, and association publications, there are specialized publications such as *Golf Shop Operations* (published by *Golf Digest/The New York Times), Golf Range And Recreation Report (The Golf Range and Recreation Association of America)* and *P.G.A. Magazine (The Professsional Golfers Association of America)*.

   Newsletters are another burgeoning category in the golf publications field. Associations such as The National Golf Foundation, publisher of *Golf Market Today*, issue a variety of special-interest newsletters and bulletins. Many newsletters not funded by associations or other large backers are difficult to locate and often have a short shelf life. Two of my favorite newsletters are *Gary Galyean's Golf Letter: The Inside Report on World Golf* (established 1990) and Golf Travel: Guide for Discriminating Golfers (established 1992).

   Below is a selected list of noteworthy periodicals. Refer to the Associations section in this book for additional sources of publications and non-print media.

GOLF PERIODICALS

ARIZONA GOLF JOURNAL
7124 E. First Street
Scottsdale, AZ 85251
(602) 949-8899

ARIZONA GOLF QUARTERLY
2730 East Broadway
Suite 250
Tucson, AZ 85716
(602) 322-0895
Fax: (602) 322-9438

BACK NINE MAGAZINE
Broadmoor Golf Club
2340 Broadmoor
   Drive E.
Seattle, WA 98112
(206) 325-5600

CALIFORNIA GOLF JOURNAL
3790 El Camino Real
Suite 164
Palo Alto, CA 94306
(415) 856-4775

CLUB DIRECTOR
National Club
   Association
Washington Harbour
3050 K St. N.W.
Suite 330
Washington, DC 20007
(202) 625-2080

CLUBMAKERS' DIGEST
71 Maholm Street
Newark, OH 43055
(614) 344-1191
(800) 321-4833
Fax: (614) 344-6154

**COLORADO
FAIRWAYS MAGAZINE**
624 Morsman Drive
Fort Collins, CO
80526-3677
(303) 226-4535
Fax: (303) 226-4534

COLORADO GOLFER
1407 Larimer Square
Denver, CO 80202
(303) 770-0100

THE COUNTRY CLUB
16 Forest Street
New Canaan, CT 06840
(203) 972-3892
Fax: (203) 966-7268

EASTERN GOLFER
P.O. Box 134, W. End
Station
W. End, New Jersey 07740
(201) 222-4877

EXECUTIVE GOLFER
2171 Campus Road
Irvine, CA 92715
(714) 752-6474
Fax: (714) 752-0398

FAIRWAY
Two Park Avenue
New York, NY 10016
(212) 779-5465
Fax: (212) 779-5465

**FAIRWAYS & GREENS—
PHILADELPHIA**
P.O. Box 96
Benwyn, PA 19312
(215) 647-4692
Fax: (215) 640-3105

**FLORIDA GOLF
REPORTER**
19900 Main Street
Town Square
Suite 4
Cornelius, NC 28031
(704) 892-7272

FLORIDA GOLFER
201 S. Airport Road
Naples, FL 33942
(813) 643-4994
Fax: (813) 643-6581

FORE
Southern California Golf
Association
3740 Cahuenga Blvd.
N. Hollywood, CA 91609
(818) 980-3630
(213) 877-0901
Fax: (818) 980-1808

FORE GOLF
2 Louella Court
Wayne, PA 19087
(215) 254-9619

FRANCE GOLF
9-11-13, rue du Colonel-
Pierre-Avia
75015 Paris
France
(33) 1 46 62 20 00

**GARY GALYEAN'S
GOLF LETTER**
Box 3899
Vero Beach, FL 32964
(800) 320-6450

**GOLF CAR NEWS
MAGAZINE**
1510 N.E. 131st Street
North Miami, FL 33161
(305) 893-9600

**GOLF COLLECTORS
SOCIETY BULLETIN**
P.O. Box 20546
Dayton, OH 45420
(513) 256-2474

**GOLF COURSE
MANAGEMENT**
1421 Research Park Drive
Lawrence, KS
66049-3859
(913) 832-4490
Fax: (913) 832-4466

GOLF COURSE NEWS
7901 4th Street North
Suite 311
St. Petersburg, FL 33702
(813) 576-7077
Fax: (813) 579-9788

GOLF DEVELOPMENT MAGAZINE
250 Bel Marin Keys Boulevard
Building A
Novato, CA 94949-5702
(415) 382-2490
Fax: (415) 382-2416

GOLF DIGEST MAGAZINE
5520 Park Avenue
Trumbull, CT 06611
(203) 373-7000
Fax: (203) 373-7033

GOLF FOR WOMEN
WOFL Building
25 Skyline Drive
Lake Mary, FL 32746
(407) 333-8821

GOLF GEORGIA
2400 Herodian Way
Suite 200
Atlanta, GA 30080
(770) 933-0086

GOLF GUIDE COMPLETE DU GOLFEUR
Media Vert
20 rue Dulong
75017 Paris
France

GOLF ILLUSTRATED
5300 CityPlex Tower
2448 E. 81st Street
Tulsa, OK 74137-4207
(918) 491-6100
Fax: (918) 491-9424

GOLF ILLUSTRATED WEEKLY
Advance House
37 Millharbour
London, E14 9TX
England

GOLF INDUSTRY
915 N.E. 12th Street
Suite 2C
North Miami, FL 33161
(305) 893-8771

GOLF JOURNAL
c/o United States Golf
  Association
Far Hills, NJ 07931
(908) 234-2300
Fax: (908) 234-9687

GOLF MAGAZINE
Two Park Avenue
New York, New York
10016
(212) 779-5000
Fax: (212) 779-5465

GOLF MARKET TODAY
c/o National Golf
  Foundation
1150 S. U.S. Highway One
Jupiter, FL 33477
(407) 744-6006
Fax: (407) 744-6107

GOLF MONTHLY
PC Magazines
King's Reach Tower
Stamford Street
London, SE1 9LS
England

THE GOLF NETWORK
6230 Busch Boulevard
Suite 444
Columbus, OH 43229
(614) 433-0393
Fax: (614) 433-0905

GOLF NEWS MAGAZINE
P.O. Box 1040
Rancho Mirage, CA 92270
(619) 324-8333
Fax: (619) 324-8011

GOLF NEWS SERVICE
220 76th Street
Virginia Beach, VA 23451
(804) 425-1648
Fax: (804) 425-1649

GOLF ORANGE COUNTY
7514 Girard Avenue
Suite 338
La Jolla, CA 92037
(800) 669-6595
Fax: (619) 459-3019

GOLF PRO MAGAZINE
7 West 34th Street
New York, NY 10001
(212) 630-3738
Fax: (212) 630-4879

GOLF PRODUCT NEWS
15-22 Fair Lawn Avenue
Fair Lawn, NJ 07410
(201) 796-6031
Fax: (201) 796-4562

GOLF RANGE AND RECREATION REPORT
211 West 92nd Street
Suite 58
New York, NY 10025
(212) 481-7792

GOLF REPORTER MAGAZINE
19900 Main Street
Town Square
Suite 4
Cornelius, NC 28031
(704) 892-7272

HOME ON THE RANGE

According to Scott Marlowe, chief executive officer of Golf Data International Inc. of Rockville, Maryland, the first golf range in America was built by John Hamilton Gillespie in 1886 in Sarasota, Florida. Gillespie, an attorney, was voted mayor of Sarasota for seven terms. The son of a Scottish lawyer, Gillespie operated a general store and had various business ventures. A member of the Royal and Ancient Golf Club of St. Andrews in his native Scotland, Gillespie designed several golf courses in Florida.

Donald Ross has generally been given credit for building the first practical golf learning center, "Maniac Hill" at the Pinehurst Resort, in 1913. Prior to the advances of Gillespie and Ross, golf was usually taught on the golf course. The practice range and learning centers contributed to the golf boom in America, especially after twenty-one-year-old American amateur Francis Ouimet won the U.S. Open in 1913 at The Country Club in Brookline, Massachusetts, in a dramatic 18-hole playoff win over seasoned British professionals Ted Ray and Harry Vardon.

GOLF SAN DIEGO
7514 Girard Avenue
Suite 338
La Jolla, CA 92037
(800) 669-6595
Fax: (619) 459-3019

GOLF SHOP OPERATIONS
5520 Park Avenue
Trumbull, CT
 06611-0395
(203) 373-7232
Fax: (203) 373-7033

GOLF TODAY
650 Blair Island Road
Suite 106
Redwood City, CA 94063
(415) 306-0122
Fax: (415) 306-0120

GOLF TRAVEL:
THE GUIDE FOR
DISCRIMINATING
GOLFERS
P.O. Box 3485
Charlottesville, VA 22903
(804) 295-1200
   (800) 225-7825
Fax: (804) 296-0948

GOLF WORLD
MAGAZINE
5520 Park Avenue
Trumbull, CT 06611
(203) 373-7000

GOLF WORLD
(BRITISH VERSION)
Advance House
37 Millharbour, Isle of
   Dogs
London, E14 9TX
England

GOLFER'S GUIDE
P.O. Box 5926
Hilton Head Island, SC
   29938-9790
(803) 842-7878
Fax: (803) 842-5743
(publisher of regional golf
guides)

THE GOLFER NEWS
MAGAZINE
660 Rockside Road
Cleveland, OH 44131
(216) 749-4436

GOLFING
IN THE OHIO SUN
660 Rockside Road
Cleveland, OH 44131
(216) 749-4436

GOLFSOUTH
P.O. Box 1899
Stone Mountain, GA
   30086
(800) 833-7540
Fax: (404) 879-5874

GOLFWEEK
7657 Commerce Center
   Drive
Orlando, FL 32819
(407) 345-5500
Fax: (407) 345-9945

GREEN SECTION
RECORD
United States Golf
   Association
Far Hills, NJ 07931
(908) 234-2300

GULF COAST GOLFER
9182 Old Katy Road
Suite 212
Houston, TX 77055
(713) 464-0308

GREAT GOLF RESORTS
OF THE WORLD
111 Presidential
   Boulevard
Suite 222
Bala Cynwyd, PA 19004
(610) 668-3564

GREENKEEPER
INTERNATIONAL
Aldwark Manor
Aldwark Aline
York YO6 2NF
England
(44) 03473-5812

LANDSCAPE
MANAGEMENT
7500 Old Oak Boulevard
Cleveland, OH 44130
(216) 826-2830
Fax: (216) 891-2675

LINKS
Southern Links
 Magazine Publishing
1040 William Hilton
 Parkway
Hilton Head Island,
 SC 29928
(803) 842-6200

METRO GOLF
2300 N. St. N.W.
Suite 600
Washington, DC 20037
(202) 663-9015
Fax: (202) 663-9015

MET GOLFER
Metropolitan Golf
 Association
125 Spencer Place
Mamaroneck, NY 10543
(914) 698-0390

**THE MICHIGAN
GOLFER**
7990 W. Grand River
Suite C
Brighton, MI 48116
(313) 227-4200

MICHIGAN GOLF NEWS
33525 Kelly Road
Clinton Township, MI
 48035
(313) 792-9800
Fax: (313) 792-9805

**MINNESOTA
FAIRWAYS MAGAZINE**
P.O. Box 21-100
St. Paul, MN 55121
(612) 681-9371

MINNESOTA GOLFER
1022 W. 80th Street
Minneapolis, MN 55420
(612) 881-3183
Fax: (602) 881-2172

**MINNESOTA
GOLF MAGAZINE**
1494 Valley Drive
Burnsville, MN 55337
(612) 890-7037
(800) 551-6690
Fax: (612) 895-9768

NATIONAL GOLFER
Heritage Publishing Co.
1324 North Rock Hill
St. Louis, MO 63124
(314) 961-8189

MYRTLE BEACH GOLF
P.O. Box 406
Myrtle Beach, SC 29578
(803) 626-0245
(800) 568-1800

NORTH TEXAS GOLFER
9182 Old Katy Road
Houston, TX 77055
(713) 464-0308

NCGA NEWS
Northern California Golf
 Association
3200 Lopez Road
Pebble Beach, CA 93953
(408) 625-4653

ON THE GREEN
P.O. Box 1463
N. Myrtle Beach, SC
29582
(803) 272-8150
Fax: (803) 272-2460

PAR EXCELLANCE
10401 W. Lincoln Avenue
West Allis, WI 53227
(414) 327-7707

PGA MAGAZINE
2155 Butterfield
Suite 200
Troy, MI 48084
(313) 649-1110
Fax: (313) 649-2306

**ROCHESTER GOLF
WEEK & SPORTS
LEDGER**
2535 Brighton-Henrietta
 Town Line Road
Rochester, NY 14623
(716) 427-2160

Popular online services such as Compuserve, Prodigy, and America Online provide access to golf discussion groups (Usenet Group Rec. Sport. Golf) as well as online versions of golf periodicals and other products. Contact: America Online (800) 827-6364; Compuserve (800) 848-8199; Prodigy Services (800) 776-3449; Microsoft Network (800) 386-5550.

In order to surf the Internet, you'll need access through personal computer, modem, and national software access providers such as Netcom (800) 3563-6600, PSI (800) 827-7482, and Alternet (800) 488-6383. Golf Data Online (GDOL) can be accessed by entering the Uniform Resource Locator (http:/www. gdol.com/index. html). GDOL is a commercial service dedicated to golf. Other sites for golf infromation include the Princeton University Golf Archives (http: // dunkin. princeton. edu); Dartmouth University (http: // ausg. dartmouth. edu / ~ pete / golf/); and Yahoo Golf Page (http: / / akebono. stanford. edu / yahoo/ entertainment / sports / golf/). Resorts such as Wild Dunes and a variety of golf organizations are on the Net, as are international golf sources such as Glasgow University, which serves as a gateway to European golf news, European Tour stats, and information on Scotish golf courses and vacation packages. Other handy services include The Masters (http: //wwwcris.com.80/Masters/); Golfplex (http://www.directnet.com/wow/golf/index.htm); Golfweb (http://wwwgolfweb.com/); The 19th Hole (http: /ww.sport.net/golf/); Unisys (http://www.unisys.com/); Golf Data Web (http: //www. gdol.com/).

By the time you read this, the Internet will be more easily accessible and a wide range of golf information including discussion groups, tour package information, handicap computation data, golf news, and other topics of interest will be more readily available.

SCORE
287 MacPherson Avenue
Toronto, Ontario
  M4V 1A4
Canada
(416) 928-2909

SENIOR GOLFER
55 Corporate Drive
Trumbull, CT 06611
(203) 459-5910
Fax: (203) 459-5199

SOUTHERN GOLFER
3023 Eastland Boulevard
Suite 103
Clearwater, FL 34621
(813) 796-3877
Fax: (813) 791-4126

SUBURBAN GOLFER
Gannett Suburban News-
  papers
1 Gannett Drive
White Plains, NY 10604
(914) 694-5038

**TEE TIME
MAGAZINE**
6935 Wisconsin Avenue
Suite 306
Chevy Chase, MD 20815
(301) 913-0081
Fax: (301) 907-6987

TODAY'S GOLFER
EMAP Pursuit
  Publishing
Bretton Court
Bretton, Peterborough
  PE3 8DZ
England
(44) 0733 264666
Fax: (44) 0733 267198

TOUR
Two Park Avenue
New York, New York
  10016
(212) 779-5000
Fax: (212) 779-5465

TURFGRASS FACTS
The Turf Resource
  Center
c/o American Sod
  Producers Association
1855-A Hicks Road
Rolling Meadows, IL
  60008
(708) 705-9898
(800) 405-8873
Fax: (708) 705-8347

**WASHINGTON
GOLF MONTHLY**
3600 New York Avenue
  N.E.
Washington, DC 20002
(202) 636-3372
Fax: (202) 526-4237

**WISCONSIN
GOLF MAGAZINE**
2317 International Lane
Suite 117
P.O. Box 14439
Madison, WI 53704
(608) 244-2600
Fax: 244-2603

7
golf videos

The advent of the videocassette recorder in the 1980s and the release of Bobby Jones's classic instructional films, produced by Warner Brothers in 1931, led to the popularity of golf on video. Jones, the consummate gentleman amateur and a hero of The Golden Age of Sport in the 1920s, retired in 1930, after completing his Grand Slam at the age of twenty-eight. Free to pursue golf commercial ventures, Jones traveled to Hollywood and filmed eighteen classic instructional shorts with movie stars such as Jimmy Cagney, W.C. Fields, Loretta Young, and Walter Huston as the obliging pupils. Jones's films also include highlights of his Grand Slam victories in the British Open, British Amateur, U.S. Open, and U.S. Amateur, a feat never equalled.

Since the mid-1980s, there has been a landslide of golf videos, including revivals of digitally mastered Shell's Wonderful World of Golf programs telecast from golf venues all over the world during the 1960s. This series features matches including Sam Snead, Arnold Palmer, Byron Nelson, Gene Sarazen, Gary Player, Billy Casper, Peter Thomson, Chi Chi Rodriguez, and other favorites in two- or three-man contests. This made-for- television series foreshadowed current popular events such as the Skins games.

Tournament videos on the Ryder Cup series, the Masters, Curtis Cup, LPGA events, PGA contests, and USGA-sponsored events such as the U.S. Open are now available. And of course there are numerous videos on golf history, junior golf, great golf courses, comedy, instruction, and specialized topics such as golf etiquette, golf for lefthanders, women's golf, physical conditioning, and others.

Virtually every golf guru and swingmeister has issued instructional films. Among these are Jack Nicklaus, David Leadbetter, Tom Watson, Ben Crenshaw, Nick Faldo, Judy Rankin, Jim McLean, Harvey Penick, Peggy Kirk Bell, Jim Flick, Nancy Lopez, Johnny Miller, Lee Trevino, Ray Floyd, Patty Sheehan, Joanne Carner, Kathy Whitworth, Ken Venturi, and many others. Perhaps you have read instructional books or articles by many of these professionals and have a favorite of your own. Should you need some comic relief, *Caddyshack* featuring Bill Murray, Chevy Chase, and Rodney Dangerfield, or Leslie Nielsen's *Bad Golf Made Easier* may amuse you.

Golf videos are available at your local pro shop or video store, the library, the United States Golf Association, or through mail-order distributors such as GolfSmart, which specializes in golf books and videos. If possible, it is better to preview these videos before you elect to purchase them. Technical quality, presentation, and relevance to your own needs can vary tremendously among any group of golf videos.

A short video preview list:

GOLF VIDEOS

Instructional

AN INSIDE LOOK
Bob Toski, Jim Flick, and Peter Kostis
56 minutes. $49.95

"ARNOLD PALMER'S PLAY GREAT GOLF"
Series of four tapes: *Mastering Fundamentals, Course Strategy, The Scoring Zone, Practice Like a Pro.*
60 minutes each.
$19.98 each

THE ART OF PUTTING
Ben Crenshaw
44 minutes. $19.95

THE AZINGER WAY
Paul Azinger
55 minutes. $19.95

BETTER GOLF NOW
Ken Venturi
40 minutes. $19.95

**BILLY CASPER
GOLF BASICS**
Billy Casper
Two tapes. 30 minutes
each. $14.95 each

**BOB TOSKI TEACHES
YOU GOLF**
Bob Toski
56 minutes. $49.95

**"BOBBY JONES
INSTRUCTIONAL
SERIES"**
Two tapes: *The Full Swing*
(45 minutes), *From Tee to
Green* (60 minutes). $69.95
each

**BUILDING AND
IMPROVING YOUR
GOLF MIND, GOLF
BODY, GOLF SWING**
Mike Hebron
Two tapes. Approximately
120 minutes each. $100.00

**CHALLENGE GOLF:
HOME EDITION—
INDIVIDUALS AND
PERSONAL TEACHERS**
Peter Longo teaches the
handicapped how to play
golf. 53 minutes. $52.95

**CHALLENGE GOLF:
TEACHING EDITION—
HOSPITALS, PARK
DISTRICTS, SCHOOLS**
Instructional video adapted
for therapists, park direc-
tors, school coaches, and
other professionals.
60 minutes. $52.95

**CHI CHI'S BAG OF
TRICKS**
Chi Chi Rodriquez
60 minutes. $19.95

**DAVE STOCKTON'S
GOLF CLINIC**
Dave Stockton
79 minutes. $49.95

DIFFICULT SHOTS
Hale Irwin
60 minutes. $49.95

**EIGHTEEN TIPS FROM
18 LEGENDS OF GOLF**
Mike Souchak, Peter
Thomson, Butch Baird,
Doug Ford, Miller
Barber, Sam Snead,
Art Wall, Tommy Bolt,
Gene Littler, Don
January, Gardner
Dickinson, Doug Sanders,
Jerry Barber, Bob Goalby,
Billy Casper, Gay Brewer,
Charlie Sifford, and Julius
Boros
120 minutes. $59.95

FAULTS AND CURES
John Jacobs
58 minutes. $69.95

**FEEL YOUR WAY
TO BETTER GOLF**
Wally Armstrong
52 minutes. $12.95

**FINDING
FUNDAMENTALS**
Bob Toski and Jim Flick
26 minutes. $32.00

**FRED COUPLES:
COUPLES ON TEMPO**
Fred Couples
20 minutes. $14.95

**THE FUNDAMENTAL
GOLF SWING**
Jimmy Ballard
69 minutes. $49.95

GARY PLAYER ON GOLF
Gary Player
90 minutes. $29.95

**GENE LITTLER'S:
THE TEN BASICS**
Gene Littler
45 minutes. $21.00

THE GOLDEN TEE
Byron Nelson, Mickey
Wright, Bob Rosburg, Billy
Casper
72 minutes. $29.95

GOLF
Al Geiberger
60 minutes. $69.95

GOLF BEGINS AT 50
Gary Player
60 minutes. $29.95

GOLF CLINIC
Al Geiberger
60 minutes. $19.95

"THE GOLF DIGEST LESSONS"
Series of ten tapes: *A Swing for a Lifetime, Finding Fundamentals, Driving for Distance, Sharpen Your Short Irons, Saving Par from the Sand, Putting for Profit, When the Chips Are Down, Winning Pitch Shots, Hitting the Long Shots, Trouble Shots: Escapes.*
26 minutes each.
$19.95 each

GOLF FOR WINNERS
Hank Haney and Mark O'Meara
42 minutes. $19.95

GOLF IS MENTAL IMAGERY
Mike Austin
56 minutes. $41.95

GOLF THE MILLER WAY
Johnny Miller
30 minutes. $19.95

"GOLF MY WAY"
Jack Nicklaus
Series of five tapes: *Hit the Shots* (128 minutes), *Play the Game* (141 minutes). $59.95 each
The Full Swing (38 minutes), *Control Shots* (39 minutes), *Short Game* (44 minutes).
$19.95 each

THE GOLF SWING
Tom Weiskopf
45 minutes. $14.95

GOLF'S STROKE SAVERS
Tom Weiskopf, Mark O'Meara, and others
34 minutes. $19.95

"THE GOLF UNIVERSITY SERIES"
Ken Blanchard
Nine tapes: *Low Handicapper's Swing School, Short Game School, High Handicapper's Swing School, Mastering the Mental Game, Senior's Swing School, The "30 Ball" Practice Routine, Women's Swing School, Trouble Shots School, Junior's Swing School.* Approximately
60 minutes each.
$24.95 each

GOLF YOUR WAY
Phil Ritson
78 minutes. $23.99

"THE GREATER GOLFER IN YOU"
Dr. Gary Wiren
Series of two tapes: *Volume I* (84 minutes), *Volume II* (87 minutes). $59.95 each

GREG NORMAN: THE LONG GAME
Greg Norman
63 minutes. $19.95

GREG NORMAN: THE SHORT GAME
Greg Norman
45 minutes. $19.95

GRIP IT AND RIP IT
John Daly
40 minutes. $29.95

HOW I PLAY GOLF
Bobby Jones
180 minutes. Includes *A Golf Story* book by Charles Price. $195.00

THE JIMMY BALLARD GOLF CONNECTION
Jimmy Ballard
90 minutes. $49.95

KEYS TO CONSISTENCY
Jack Grout
59 minutes. $39.95

**KEYS TO THE
EFFORTLESS GOLF
SWING**
Michael McTeigue
80 minutes. $24.95

KING OF CLUBS
Peter Longo
40 minutes. $24.95

THE LAST 100 YARDS
Jack Grout
45 minutes. $39.95

LEARNING GOLF
Mike Calbot
90 minutes. $49.95

**"LEE TREVINO'S
PRICELESS GOLF TIPS"**
Lee Trevino
Series of three tapes: *Chipping and Putting* (25 minutes), *Getting Out of Trouble* (27 minutes), *Swing, Distance and Control* (25 minutes). $19.95

**"A LESSON WITH DAVID
LEADBETTER"**
David Leadbetter
Series of three tapes: *Taking It to the Course* (90 minutes), *The Short Game* (100 minutes), *The Full Swing* (90 minutes). $59.95 each

**MAKE EVERY SHOT
A NICE SHOT!**
Chuck Hogan
65 minutes. $19.95

**"THE MASTER SYSTEM
TO MODERN GOLF,
VOL. I"**
Series of four tapes: *Craig Stadler on the Short Game; Davis Love III on Driving; Tom Purtzer on Iron Accuracy; Gary Koch on Putting.* 20 minutes each. $14.95 each

**"THE MASTER SYSTEM
TO MODERN GOLF,
VOL. II"**
Series of three tapes: *Paul Azinger on Fairway, Sand Traps and Greens; Fred Couples on Tempo; Bobby Wadkins on Trouble Shots.* 20 minutes each. $14.95 each

**THE MASTER SYSTEM
TO BETTER GOLF:
THE SENIORS**
Miller Barber, Dale Douglas, and Orville Moody
115 minutes. $39.95

**MASTERING THE
LONG PUTTER**
John Schlee
50 minutes. $39.95

**MOST COMMON
FAULTS AND CURES**
Jim Flick
42 minutes. $19.95

**NICK FALDO'S
GOLF COURSE I**
Nick Faldo and David Leadbetter
60 minutes. $19.98

**NICK FALDO'S GOLF
COURSE II**
Nick Faldo
61 minutes. $19.98

"PGA TOUR GOLF"
Hal Sutton, Craig Stadler, Lanny Wadkins, Payne Stewart,
Tom Kite.
Series of three tapes:
The Full Swing, The Short Game, Course Strategy. 60 minutes each. $19.98 each

PLAY YOUR BEST GOLF
Tommy Armour.
Includes book
38 minutes. $39.95

"PLAY YOUR BEST GOLF"
Bob Toski, Jim Flick, Conrad Rehling, Gary Wiren, Peggy Kirk Bell, Rod Meyers, Carol Johnson
Series of two tapes: *Volume I, The Clubs* (69 minutes), *Volume II, The Strategies* (109 minutes). $29.95 each

THE PLAYER'S COURSE
Chuck Hogan with Johnny Miller, Peter Jacobsen, and Mike Reid Two videos, four audios, two manuals. $147.00

POWERBALL
David Leadbetter
Tape with instructional booklet. $39.95

POWER DRIVING
Mike Dunaway
30 minutes. $49.95

POWER GAME
Ian Woosnam
55 minutes. $19.98

PRECISION PUTTING
Dave Stockton
30 minutes. $49.95

PUTT FOR DOUGH AND HOW TO READ GREENS
Lee Trevino
50 minutes. $19.95

PUTT LIKE THE PROS
Dave Pelz
34 minutes. $29.95

"REACHING YOUR GOLF POTENTIAL"
Tom Kite
Series of two tapes: *Developing Maximum Consistency* (50 minutes), *Strategies and Techniques* (60 minutes). $19.95 each

RICK SMITH'S SIGNATURE SERIES— RANGE TIPS
Rick Smith
$39.95

SAVING PAR FROM THE SAND
Sam Snead
60 minutes. $49.95

SCRAMBLE FOR BETTER GOLF
Fuzzy Zoeller
42 minutes. $19.95

SECRETS FOR SENIORS
Sam Snead
60 minutes. $39.95

SHARPEN YOUR SHORT IRONS
Jim Flick
26 minutes. $32.00

THE SHORT GAME
Seve Ballesteros
65 minutes. $19.95

"THE SHORT WAY TO LOWER SCORING"
Paul Runyan
Series of two tapes: *Putting and Chipping* (35 minutes), *Pitching and Sand Play* (26 minutes). $19.95 each

SIXTY YARDS IN
Ray Floyd
60 minutes. $39.95

STROKE SAVERS
Ken Venturi
59 minutes. $24.95

SUPER POWER GOLF
Dr. Gary Wiren
55 minutes. $19.95

A SWING FOR A LIFETIME
Bob Toski and Jim Flick 26 minutes. $32.00

THE SWING MOTION
George Knudson
25 minutes. $24.95

TEN FUNDAMENTALS OF THE MODERN GOLF SWING
David Glenz and Jim McLean
32 minutes. $19.95

TIPS FROM THE TOUR
Corey Pavin, Nick Price
and nine others
35 minutes. $14.95

**TOTAL PUTTING
GUIDE**
Bob Rosberg
29 Minutes. $19.95

WINNING GOLF
Al Geiberger
60 minutes. $29.95

WIN AND WIN AGAIN
Curtis Strange
60 minutes. $19.95

THE X-FACTOR
Jim McClean
50 minutes. $39.95

Women's Golf

**BEGINNING GOLF
FOR WOMEN**
Donna White
45 minutes. $14.95

GOLF
Patty Sheehan
60 minutes. $69.95

GOLF MADE EASY
Nancy Lopez
48 minutes. $29.95

GOLF REVOLUTION
Jan Stephenson
60 minutes. $29.95

HOW TO GOLF
Jan Stephenson
50 minutes. $29.95

THE KEYS TO GOLF
Joanne Carner
90 minutes. $39.95

PRACTICE TEE
Judy Rankin
28 minutes. $19.95

WINNING AT GOLF
Amy Alcott
37 minutes. $14.95

"WOMEN'S GOLF"
Peggy Kirk Bell, Dede
Owens, and others
Series of two tapes:
*The Full Swing, The
Approach Game.*
40 minutes each.
$19.95 each

**THE WOMEN'S GOLF
GUIDE**
Helene Landers
For beginning golfers.
59 minutes. $19.95

Junior Golf

**GOLF FOR KIDS
OF ALL AGES**
Wally Armstrong and
"Gabby Gator" (cartoon
character)
50 minutes. $14.95

**LEE TREVINO'S GOLF
TIPS FOR YOUNGSTERS**
Lee Trevino
40 minutes. $19.95

**NICK FALDO'S JUNIOR
MASTER CLASS**
Nick Faldo
70 minutes. $19.95

SCHOLASTIC GOLF
Eric Alpenfels and Jay
Haas
47 minutes. $19.95

Golf Courses

**COURSES OF
PEBBLE BEACH**
54 minutes. $29.95

**GREAT GOLF COURSES
OF THE WORLD:
SCOTLAND**
Sean Connery and Jack
Nicklaus
77 minutes. $29.95

**"CLASSIC GOLF
EXPERIENCES: A
PLAYER'S GUIDE TO
THE COURSES"**
Series of three tapes:
*Doral's Blue Monster, Bay
Course at Kapalua, St.
Andrews Old Course.*
45 minutes each.
$14.95 each

Golf Comedies

**BAD GOLF
MADE EASIER**
Leslie Nielsen
40 minutes. $19.98

CADDYSHACK
Movie with Bill Murray,
Chevy Chase, and
others
90 minutes. $29.95

DORF GOLF BIBLE
Tim Conway
36 minutes. $14.95

DORF ON GOLF
Tim Conway
30 minutes. $14.95

**GOLF'S GOOF-UPS
AND MIRACULOUS
MOMENTS**
Robert Wahl
45 minutes. $19.95

I HATE THIS GAME
Thom Sharp
40 minutes. $19.95

**JUST MISSED . . . .
DAMMIT!**
40 minutes. $19.95

**LITTLE SCAMS ON
GOLF**
Rich Little
Impersonations.
44 minutes. $14.95

Miscellany

ETIQUETTE OF GOLF
Tim Brandt
35 minutes. $19.95

**EXERCISES
FOR BETTER GOLF**
Corey Pavin,
Peter Jacobsen, and
Dr. Frank Jobe
73 minutes. $29.95

**GOLF FROM THE
OTHER SIDE**
Bob Charles
59 minutes. $49.95

**GOLF'S GAMBLING
GAMES**
Gary McCord and friends
55 minutes. $19.95

**GOOD GOLF
FOR BAD BACKS**
Dr. Gary Wiren with neu-
rological surgeon Dr.
Jordan Grabel
$24.95

**RULES OF GOLF
EXPLAINED**
Tom Watson
23 minutes. $13.95

**STRETCHING
THE DRIVING FORCE**
Warmup routine.
19 minutes. $14.95

**USGA RULES OF GOLF
ON VIDEO**
Indexed. 84 minutes.
$24.95

**VIDEO GUIDE TO GOLF
ETIQUETTE**
Payne Stewart
30 minutes $19.95

History and Memorabilia

**THE BEST OF
BOBBY JONES**
Bobby Jones
Instructional tape,
Triumphant Journey (book),
sleeve of golf balls.
70 minutes. $99.95

**FOLLOW THE SUN:
THE BEN HOGAN
STORY**
Glenn Ford in the
feature-length film.
96 minutes. $19.95

**GOLDEN GREATS
OF GOLF**
Peter Dobereiner.
60 minutes $29.95

**GOLF'S GREATEST
MOMENTS**
77 minutes. $29.98

GOLF MEMORIES
Bobby Jones, W. C. Fields,
Bob Hope,
Gene Sarazen, and many
others
60 minutes. $41.95

**"THE HISTORY OF
GOLF"**
Series of four tapes
280 minutes. $119.98

**JACK NICKLAUS SHOWS
YOU THE GREATEST
18 HOLES IN
CHAMPIONSHIP GOLF**
Jack Nicklaus
65 minutes. $19.95

LEGACY OF THE LINKS
Lee Trevino at St. Andrews
90 minutes. $19.95

**TOM MORRIS, KEEPER
OF THE GREENS**
63 minutes. $19.95

**SHELL'S WONDERFUL
WORLD OF GOLF**
Vol. 1 Cotton and Sarazen
at St. Andrews
Vol. 2 DeVicenzo and
Lema at Glyfada Golf
Club in Athens, Greece

Vol. 3 Littler and
Nelson at Pine Valley in
New Jersey
Vol. 4 Palmer and Boros at
Cotton Bay Club in the
Bahamas
Vol. 5 Demaret and Snead
at Eisenhower Golf
Course in
Colorado
Vol. 6 Brewer, Palmer, and
Rodriguez at El Con-
quistador in Puerto Rico
Vol. 7 DeVicenzo and
Snead at Congressional
Country Club in Mary-
land

Vol. 8 Allis and Lema at
the Mid-Ocean Club in
Bermuda
Vol. 9 Beard, Boros, and
Trevino at Club de Golf
in Mexico
Vol. 10 Rodriguez and
Souchak at Panama
Country Club in
Panama
Vol. 11 Boros and Snead at
Peachtree Golf Club in
Georgia
Vol. 12 Player and Thom-
son at Royal Melbourne
in Australia

THE URBAN GOLFER

Not far from the traffic of Wacker and Lake Shore Drive in Chicago is the 9-hole par-27 Illinois Center Golf which also has a driving range. The par-3 holes on the short course range from 57 yards to 145 yards in length, and it usually takes about seventy minutes (and a $22 green fee) to play a round. The fee for a bucket of range balls is $9. The facility has a 5,000-square-foot putting green, two sand bunkers, and 125 driving slots. Memberships, lessons, and discount plans are available.

Contact: Illinois Center Golf, 221 N. Columbus, Chicago, IL 60601, (312) 616-1234. Hours are from 6:60 A.M. to 8:30 P.M. daily, year round.

Vol. 13 Palmer, Sanders, and Beard at PGA National Golf Club in Florida

Vol. 14 Nelson and de Wit at Haagshe Golf Club in the Netherlands

Vol. 15 Brewer and Casper at the Doral Golf Club in Florida

Vol. 16 Sanders and Alliss at Penina Golf Club in Portugal

Vol. 17 Ching-Po and Lema at Kawana Golf Club in Japan

Vol. 18 Stockton, Weiskopf, and DeVicenzo at Rangelagh Golf Club in Argentina

Vol. 19 Goalby and Charles at Paraparamu Beach Golf Club in New Zealand

Vol. 20 Whitworth, Mann, and Haynie at Royal Bangkok Sports Club in Thailand

"Shell's Wonderful World of Golf" series was filmed in 50 countries and aired from 1962 to 1970. Additional videos will be released. Each video is approximately 55 minutes long, covering an 18-hole match between some of the world's best golfers. The original footage has been digitally remastered, and each video is priced at $24.95

USGA Events

USGA GIRLS' JUNIOR VIDEO $4.50

1956 U.S. Open won by Cary Middlecoff at Oak Hill Country Club, Rochester, New York. 17 minutes. $19.95

1962 U.S. Open won by Jack Nicklaus at Oakmont Country Club, Oakmont, Pennsylvania. 33 minutes. $19.95

1963 U.S. Open won by Julius Boros at the Country Club in Brookline, Massachusetts. 39 minutes. $19.95

1964 U.S. Open won by Ken Venturi at Congressional Country Club, Bethesda, Maryland, 32 minutes. $19.95

1965 U.S. Open won by Gary Player at Bellerive Country Club, St. Louis, Missouri. 36 minutes. $19.95

1966 U.S. Open won by Billy Casper at Olympic Country Club, San Francisco, California. 40 minutes. $19.95

1967 U.S. Open won by Jack Nicklaus at Baltusrol Golf Club, Springfield, New Jersey. 39 minutes. $19.95

1968 U.S. Open won by Lee Trevino at Oak Hill Country Club, Rochester, New York. 39 minutes. $19.95

1969 U.S. Open win by Orville Moody at Champions Golf Club, Houston, Texas. 37 minutes. $19.95

1970 U.S. Open won by Tony Jacklin at Hazeltine National Golf Club, Chaska, Minnesota. 33 minutes. $19.95

1971 U.S. Open won by Lee Trevino at Merion Golf Club, Ardmore, Pennsylvania. 34 minutes. $19.95

1972 U.S. Open won by Jack Nicklaus at Pebble Beach Golf Links, Pebble Beach, California. 30 minutes. $19.95

1973 U.S. Open won by Johnny Miller at Oakmont Country Club, Oakmont,Pennsylvania. 31 minutes. $19.95

1974 U.S. Open won by Hale Irwin at Winged Foot Golf Club, Mamaroneck, New York. 32 minutes. $19.95

1975 U.S. Open won by Lou Graham at Medinah Country Club, Medinah, Illinois. 30 minutes. $19.95

1976 U.S. Open won by Jerry Pate at Atlantic Athletic Club, Duluth, Georgia. 27 minutes. $19.95

1977 U.S. Open won by Hubert Green at Southern Hills Country Club, Tulsa, Oklahoma. 36 minutes. $19.95

1978 U.S. Open won by Andy North at Cherry Hills Country Club, Englewood, Colorado. 26 minutes. $19.95

1979 U.S. Open won by Hale Irwin at Inverness Club, Toledo, Ohio. 30 minutes. $19.95

1980 U.S. Open won by Jack Nicklaus at Baltusrol Golf Club, Springfield, New Jersey. 40 minutes. $19.95

1981 U.S. Open won by David Graham at Merion Golf Club, Ardmore, Pennsylvania. 36 minutes. $19.95

1982 U.S. Open won by Tom Watson at Pebble Beach Golf Links, Pebble Beach, California. 36 minutes. $19.95

1983 U.S. Open won by Larry Nelson at Oakmont Country Club, Oakmont, Pennsylvania. 36 minutes. $19.95

1984 U.S. Open won by Fuzzy Zoeller at Winged Foot Golf Club, Mamaroneck, New York. 37 minutes. $19.95

1985 U.S. Open won by Andy North at Oakland Hills Country Club, Birmingham, Michigan. 30 minutes. $19.95

1986 U.S. Open won by Raymomd Floyd at Shinnecock Hills Golf Club, Southampton, New York. 28 minutes. $19.95

1987 U.S. Open won by Scott Simpson at The Olympic Club, San Francisco, California. 59 minutes. $19.95

1988 U.S. Open won by Curtis Strange at The Country Club, Brookline, Massachusetts. 50 minutes. $19.95

1988 U.S. Women's Open won by Liselotte Neumann at Baltimore Country Club, Baltimore, Maryland. 50 minutes. $19.95

1989 U.S. Open won by Curtis Strange at Oak Hill Country Club, Rochester, New York. 55 minutes. $19.95

1989 U.S. Women's Open
won by Betsy King at Indianwood Golf and Country Club,
Lake Orion, Michigan.
53 minutes. $19.95

1990 U.S. Open won by
Hale Irwin at Medinah
Country Club, Medinah, Illinois.
60 minutes. $19.95

1990 U.S. Women's Open
won by Betsy King at Atlantic
Athletic Club, Duluth, Georgia.
53 minutes. $19.95

1991 U.S. Open won by
Payne Stewart at Hazeltine
National Golf Club, Chaska,
Minnesota.
60 minutes. $19.95

1991 U.S. Women's Open
won by Meg Mallon at the
Colonial Country Club, Fort
Worth, Texas. $19.95

1992 U.S. Open won by
Tom Kite at Pebble Beach
Golf Links, Pebble Beach,
California.
60 minutes. $19.95

1992 U.S. Senior Open
won by Larry Laoretti at
Saucon Valley Country Club,
Bethlehem,
Pennsylvania.
$19.95

1993 U.S. Open won by Lee
Janzen at Baltusrol Golf
Club, Springfield, New Jer-
sey.
$19.95

1993 U.S. Senior Open
won by Jack Nicklaus at
Cherry Hills Country Club,
Englewood,
Colorado.
$19.95

1993 U.S. Women's Open
won by Lauri Merten at
Crooked Stick, Carmel, Indiana.
$19.95

1994 U.S. Amateur won by
Eldrick "Tiger" Woods at
TPC Sawgrass, Ponte Vedra
Beach, Florida. $19.95

1994 U.S. Open won by
Ernie Els at Oackmont
Country Club, Oakmont,
Pennsylvania.
$19.95

1994 U.S. Senior Open
won by Simon Hobday at
Pinehurst Country Club,
Pinehurst, North Carolina.
$19.95

1994 U.S. Women's Open
won by Patty Sheehan at
Indianwood Golf and Country
Club, Lake Orion, Michigan.
$19.95

**The U.S. Open Golf
Championships: 93 Years
of U.S. Open Highlights.**
60 minutes. $19.98

The Masters

1986 Jack Nicklaus
60 minutes. $19.95

1987 Larry Mize
60 minutes. $19.95

1988 Sandy Lyle
60 minutes. $19.95

1989 Nick Faldo
52 minutes. $19.95

1990 Nick Faldo
60 minutes. $19.95

The LPGA was formed after World War II and began to keep official records beginning in 1948.

• The prize money in LPGA events has increased from $50,000 in nine events in 1950 to $21,975,000 in thirty-seven events in 1994. Babe Zaharias led the LPGA in official earnings in 1950 with $14,800, or almost 30% of the total money available. Laura Davies led with $687,201 in 1994.

• Kathy Whitworth has the greatest number of officially sanctioned tour events of any golfer with 88.

• Mickey Wright holds the record for the most victories in a season with thirteen in 1963.

• Beth Daniel set the record for average score with a mark of 70.38 in 93 rounds in 1989.

• Nancy Lopez and Beth Daniel share the all-time 72-hole tournament low score with 20-under-par totals of 268.

• Nancy Lopez holds the record for consecutive wins in tournaments participated in with five in 1978.

• Mickey Wright and Kathy Whitworth share the record for consecutive wins in scheduled events—four.

• Kathy Whitworth is the first lady golfer to win $1 million on tour. She did it in 1981 after she had won eighty-one tournaments. Brandie Burton reached the same plateau at the age of twenty-one years, seven months and twenty-one days, after winning two events on the tour.

1991 Ian Woosnam
60 minutes. $19.95

1992 Fred Couples
52 minutes. $14.95

1993 Bernhard Langer
52 minutes. $14.95

1994 Jose Maria Olazabal
52 minutes. $14.95

Great Moments of the Masters
52 minutes. $19.95

Other Tournaments

1980 British Open: Tom Watson wins at Muirfield.
52 minutes. $19.95

1981 British Open: Phil Rogers wins at Royal St. George's.
52 minutes. $19.95

1983 British Open: Tom Watson wins at Royal Birkdale.
52 minutes. $19.95

1992 British Open: Nick Faldo wins at Muirfield. 55 minutes. $19.95

75 Years of the PGA Championship: Great Champions, Great Moments
65 minutes. $19.95

Ryder Cup 1993: Showdown at the Belfry
65 minutes. $19.95

Most of the videos listed here are available from GolfSmart, 13100 Grass Valley Avenue, Grass Valley, CA 95945, (916) 272-1556, (800) 637-3557. For USGA tapes, contact the USGA, P.O. Box 708, Far Hills, NJ 07931, (908) 724-4600.

This is a rather befuddling topic. First of all, there seems to be little consensus regarding what constitutes a great golf course. Everyone has a list, such as "Golf Magazine's Top 100" or "Golf Digest's Top 100" and so forth. Many golfers await these lists and their objective selection criteria to see how the pecking order has changed over the years. The guidelines for compiling these lists, though seemingly unbiased, can quickly become subjective in a variety of ways. First of all, there is the matter of less-than-scientific sampling criteria (the samples are not random, and courses can stay on the elite list even if they've almost been wiped out by a hurricane). And, of course, there can be conflicts of interest and varying perspectives, abilities and golf handicaps within the judging committees. In addition, the sheer logistical complexity of assessing the merits of hundreds of golf courses may produce some subjectivity. All of this having been said, the various publications and other raters of golf courses do a reasonably good job, given the circumstances.

A true connoisseur, of course, might have some reasonably objective criteria, like those Bobby Jones and Alister Mackenzie had when they created

8

golf places to play: the quest for the best golf courses

Augusta National. Legend has it that these kindred spirits stood on a hill at what was then the Berckmans nursery and agreed on guidelines for the home of the Masters. Mackenzie had his thirteen essential features of a golf course, and among them were "There should be a complete absence of the annoyance caused by the necessity of searching for lost balls." One does not easily lose golf balls at great courses like Pinehurst No. 2, St. Andrews, Pebble Beach, Winged Foot, or Augusta National; but it is easy to lose strokes.

Of course this was a dream team of sorts. Jones had just won the Grand Slam of golf, a feat never equalled, and he was the best shotmaker in the world. Jones had the first-hand experience of having played the best golf courses, including St. Andrews, Winged Foot, Cypress Point, and many others. He also had degrees in engineering (Georgia Tech) and literature (Havard); and, after attending Emory University, he practiced law. Alister Mackenzie graduated from Cambridge University with degrees in medicine, natural science, and history. In 1920, Mackenzie published the first classic on golf-course architecture, *Golf Architecture: Economy in Course Construction and Greenkeeping*. Notable earlier books related to golf-course design were *Famous Golf Links* (1891), an account of the best golf courses in Great Britain by Horace Hutchinson, and Bernard Darwin's *The Great Golf Courses of the British Isles*, published in 1910.

Jones wrote his own classic, his autobiography *Down The Fairway* in collaboration with O. B. Keeler. This book, considered by many to be the best golf book ever written, was released in 1927 when Jones was twenty-five years of age. By the time Jones and Mackenzie teamed up at Augusta, Mackenzie had designed many golf courses including the Cypress Point Club with Robert Hunter (1928), the Royal Melbourne West Course with Alex Russell (1931), and other classics. Jones and Mackenzie were superbly matched to be kindred spirits in golf.

Augusta National is splendidly etched into a welcoming, verdant arboretum. People have begged, borrowed, or stolen trying to get a tee time at this exclusive club, the home of the Masters rite of spring. Jones said he would like to play the Old Course at St. Andrews if he had to choose a place to play one final round. Others have referred to that venerable linksland as a "goat pasture," which it might seem to the untutored the first few times around. Jack Nicklaus claims that Pebble Beach is the place to tee it up for the last time. Others would vote for Pine Valley, Cypress Point, Shinnecock, or a few others. These are considered to be among the classic layouts, like the creations of Rembrandt, Michelangelo, or Botticelli.

Golf-course architecture has gradually become a mix of art, commerce, and high technology. H. S. Colt and C. H. Alison wrote *Some Essays on Golf-Course Architecture* (1920); Robert Hunter wrote *The Links* (1926), and George C. Thomas followed with *Golf Architecture in America: Its Strategy and Construction* in 1927. Then Charles Blair Macdonald, designer of the Chicago Golf Club course and the National Golf Links in Southampton, Long Island, weighed in with *Scotland's Gift—Golf* the following year. Since then, notable books such as *The Architecture of Golf* by Geoffrey Cornish and Ronald E. Whitten [an expanded edition of their *The Golf Course* (1981)]; *The World Atlas of Golf* edited by Pat-Ward Thomas, Herbert Warren Wind, Charles Price, and Peter Thomson (first issued in 1976 and since updated); *The Anatomy of a Golf Course* (1992) by Tom Doak, and other excellent books on golf-course design and construction have been published.

But still among the best courses in the world are those designed entirely or in part by amateurs. The classic examples are The Old Course at St. Andrews, Pine Valley (1922), designed by George Crump with routing by H. S. Colt and completed by Hugh Wilson after Mr. Crump's death in 1918; Pebble Beach (1918) by Jack Neville and Douglas S. Grant; and Oakmont (1904) by Henry C. Fownes and William C. Fownes, Jr. Oakmont and Pine Valley are heavily penal golf courses that often allow little choice about routes to target areas. Augusta, Saint Andrews, and Pebble Beach are more strategic in design, with a variety of avenues to the target but penalties for choosing easier routes to the hole.

There are some golfers roaming this earth like Ulysses trying to play the "best" golf courses in the world. For those we have a select international list of fifty that might be difficult to reach and, even if you do, there might be a guard on duty akin to the police station adjacent to the front gate at Pine Valley. We'll call these the "Dream 50" because image is everything.

The second list includes over 225 places and more than three hundred courses in North America and the nearby islands where you can play without a membership. We'll call these the "People's 300 Plus" for marketing purposes. Among this accessible group are Pinehurst No. 2, Pebble Beach, Kiawah's Ocean Course,

Kemper Lakes, Bay Hill, Doral's Blue Course, Pasatiempo, Blackwolf Run, The Golden Horseshoe, The Broadmoor, TPC Sawgrass, Harbour Town, Wild Dunes Links Course, and many other fine venues. The sad part is that there are so many golf courses and so little time.

THE DREAM 50

Many of these courses, especially the ones in the British Isles, are accessible to the public. Consult with your professional or the tour services listed in the travel section of this book.

AUGUSTA NATIONAL GOLF CLUB
Augusta, Georgia, U.S.A., 18/6,904/72*

Alister Mackenzie with Bobby Jones (1932). Remodeled by Perry Maxwell (1937), Robert Trent Jones (1946 and 1950), George W.Cobb (1967), George W. Cobb and John L. Foy (1977), George Fazio (1972), Joseph S. Finger and Byron Nelson (1979), Jay Morrish and Bob Cupp (1980), and Jack Nicklaus (1985).

BALTUSROL GOLF CLUB

Springfield, New Jersey, U.S.A., Lower Course, 18/7,022/72

A. W. Tillinghast (1922). Remodeled by Robert Trent Jones (1952) and Rees Jones (1992).

BALLYBUNION GOLF CLUB
Ballybunion, Ireland, Old Course, 18/6,542/72

P. Murphy (1906). James Braid and John R. Stutt remodeled 9, with an additional 9 (1927); remodeled by Tom Simpson with Molly Gourlay (1936).

CARNOUSTIE GOLF CLUB
Tayside, Scotland, Championship Course, 18/7,200/72

Allan Robertson (1842). Remodeled by Willie Park, Jr., and Old Tom Morris; Additional 9 by Old Tom Morris (1867). Remodeled by James Braid and John R. Stutt (1926,1936).

CASA DE CAMPO
La Romana, Dominican Republic, Teeth of the Dog Course, 18/6,888/72,

Pete Dye (1971) .

CHICAGO GOLF CLUB
Wheaton, Illinois, U.S.A., 18/6,553/70

C. B. Macdonald (1895). Remodeled by Seth Raynor (1926).

COLONIAL COUNTRY CLUB
Fort Worth, Texas, U.S.A., 18/7,142/72

John Bredemus (1935). Additional 3, Perry Maxwell (1939).

* Numbers indicate number of holes/total yardage/par.

THE COUNTRY CLUB
Brookline, Massachusetts,
U.S.A., Open Course,
18/7,010/71

Willie Campbell 1893.
Additional 3, Willie Camp-
bell (1895). Remodeled,
with an additional 9,
William S. Flynn (1927).
Remodeled by Geoffrey S.
Cornish (1960), Geoffrey
S. Cornish and William G.
Robinson (1969), and Rees
Jones (1985).

**CRYSTAL DOWNS
COUNTRY CLUB,**
Frankfort,
Michigan, U.S.A.,
18/6,518/70

Alister Mackenzie and
Perry Maxwell (1933).
Remodeled by Geoffrey
Cornish and Brian Silva
(1985).

CYPRESS POINT CLUB
Pebble Beach, California,
U.S.A., 18/6,464/72

Alister Mackenzie with
Robert Hunter (1928).

**DURBAN
COUNTRY CLUB**
Durban, South Africa,
18/6,576/72

Laurie Waters and George
Waterman (1920). Remod-
eled by S. V. Hotchkin
(1928).

**FISHERS ISLAND
GOLF CLUB**
Fishers Island, New York,
U.S.A., 18/6,445/72

Seth Raynor (1917).

**GARDEN CITY
GOLF CLUB**
Garden City, New York,
U.S.A., 18/6,840/72

Devereaux Emmet (1899).
Remodeled by Walter J.
Travis and Robert Trent
Jones (1935, 1958).

THE GOLF CLUB
New Albany, Ohio, U.S.A.,
18/7,037/72

Pete Dye (1967).

**HIRONO COUNTRY
CLUB**
Kobe, Japan, 18/6,566/72

C. H. Alison (1932).

INVERNESS CLUB
Toledo, Ohio, U.S.A.,
18/6,982/71

Bernard Nicholls. Remod-
eled with an additional 9,
by Donald Ross (1919).
Remodeled by A. W. Till-
inghast (1930), Dick Wil-
son (1956), Robert Bruce
Harris (1957), Arthur Hills
(1970), George and Tom
Fazio, with an additional 9
(1978), Arthur Hills (1983).

KINGSTON HEATH
Melbourne, Australia,
18/6,814/72

Des Soutar (1925). Remod-
eled by Alister Mackenzie
(1928) and Peter Thomson
and Michael Wolveridge.

**LOS ANGELES
COUNTRY CLUB**
Los Angeles, California,
U.S.A., North Course,
18/6,811/72

George Thomas, Jr. (1911).
Remodeled by Wiilam P.
Bell (1928) and Robert
Muir Graves (1982).

MEDINAH COUNTRY CLUB
Medinah, Illinois, Course No. 3, 18/7,365/72

Tom Bendelow (1929). Remodeled, with an additional 5, by Harry Collis (1932), with an additional 2, by Roger Packard (1986). Remodeled by Bob Lohmann (1986).

MERION GOLF CLUB
Ardmore, Pennsylvania, U.S.A., East Course, 18/6,544/70

Hugh Wilson (1912). Remodeled by William S. Flynn and Howard Toomey (1925), Perry Maxwell (1939), Dick Wilson (1965).

MUIRFIELD GOLF CLUB
Muirfield, Lothian, Scotland, 18/6,894/71

Old Tom Morris. Remodeled additional 7 by H. S. Colt and C. S. Alison (1925) and Tom Simpson (1933).

MUIRFIELD VILLAGE GOLF CLUB
Dublin, Ohio, 18/7,106/72

Jack Nickalaus and Desmond Muirhead (1974).

NATIONAL GOLF LINKS OF AMERICA
Southampton, New York, U.S.A., 18/6,745/72

Charles Blair Macdonald (1911). Remodeled by Perry Maxwell (1939) and Robert Trent Jones (1948 and 1969).

OAK HILL COUNTRY CLU
Rochester, New York, U.S.A., East Course, 18/6,964/70

Donald Ross (1926). Remodeled by Robert Trent Jones (1956, 1967). Remodeled, with an additional 3, by George and Tom Fazio (1973).

OAKMONT COUNTRY CLUB
Oakmont, Pennsylvania, U.S.A., 18/6,989/71

William and Henry Fownes (1903). Remodeled by William C. Fownes, Jr., and Emil Loeffler (1920), Arthur Jack Snyder (1952), Robert Trent Jones (1964), Arnold Palmer and Ed Seay (1978), Ferdinand Garbin (1983), and Arthur Hills (1988).

OAKLAND HILLS COUNTRY CLUB
Birmingham, Michigan, U.S.A., South Course, 18/7,067/72

Donald Ross (1918). Remodeled by Robert Trent Jones (1950, 1972, and 1984) and Arthur Hills (1987).

OLYMPIC CLUB
San Francisco, California, U.S.A., Lake Course, 18/6,748/71

Wilfrid Watson (1924). Remodeled by Max Behr (1926), Sam Whiting, and Robert Trent Jones (1954).

**PINE VALLEY
GOLF CLUB**
Clementon, New Jersey,
U.S.A., 18/6,765/72

George Crump and H. S.
Colt (1914). Additional 4,
Hugh and Alan Wilson
(1922). Remodeled by
William S. Flynn (1929),
Perry Maxwell (1933), and
Tom Fazio (1989).

**PORTMARNOCK
GOLF CLUB**
Portmarnock, Ireland, Old
Course, 18/7,103/72

George W. Ross and W. C.
Pikeman (1894). Remod-
eled by Henry M. Cairnes;
H. S. Colt (additional 1,
remodeled 3, 1919) ; Eddie
Hackett, and Fred Hawtree
(additional 9, 1964).

**PRAIRIE DUNES
COUNTRY CLUB**
Hutchinson, Kansas,
U.S.A., 18/6,542/70

Perry Maxwell (1937).
Additional 9, Press
Maxwell (1977). Remod-
eled by Bill Coore and Ben
Crenshaw (2 holes, 1989).

**QUAKER RIDGE
COUNTRY CLUB**
Scarsdale, New York,
U.S.A., 70/6,745/70

John Duncan Dunn (9
holes, 1915). Remodeled
with an additional 9, A. W.
Tillinghast (1926). Remodeled by Robert Trent Jones
(1962) and Frank Duane
(1964).

**RIVIERA
COUNTRY CLUB**
Pacific Palisades,
California, U.S.A.,
18/7,101/72

George Thomas, Jr., and
William P. Bell (1926).

**ROYAL BIRKDALE
GOLF CLUB**
Southport, Merseyside,
England, 18/7,001/72

George Low and Charles
Hawtree (1889). Remod-
eled by F. G. Hawtree and
J. H. Taylor (1932)
Fred W. Hawtree (1967
and 1974), D.M.A. Steel
(additional 2, 1987).

**ROYAL COUNTRY
DOWN GOLF CLUB**
Newcastle, Down,
Northern Ireland,
18/6,995/72

Old Tom Morris (1891).
Remodeled by C. S.
Butchart, Seymour Dunn
(1905), and Harry Vardon
(1908, 1919).

**ROYAL DORNOCH
GOLF CLUB**
Dornoch, Highland,
Scotland, 18/6,533/70

Old Tom Morris (9, 1887).
Remodeled, with an addi-
tional 9, John Sutherland,
J. H. Taylor (1907); Don-
ald Ross (additional 2,
1921), George Duncan
(additional 4, 1947).

**ROYAL LIVERPOOL
GOLF CLUB**
Hoylake, Merseyside,
Scotland, 18/6,979/72

Robert Chambers, Jr., and
George Morris (1869).
Remodeled by H. S. Colt
(1912 and 1920), J.J.F. Pen-
ninck (1966), Fred W.
Hawtree (1967).

ROYAL LYTHAM & ST. ANNES GOLF CLUB

St. Annes-on-Sea, Lancashire, 18/6,673/71

George Low (1897) Remodeled by Tom Simpson, Herbert Fowler, H. S. Colt, and C. H. Alison (1930), H. S. Colt and J.S.F. Morrison (12, 1923 and 5, 1932), J.S.F. Morrison; C. K. Cotton and J.J.F. Penninck (1952), D.M.A. Steel (1987).

ROYAL ST. GEORGE'S GOLF CLUB

Sandwich, England, 18/6,829/72

W. Laidlaw Purves (1887). Remodeled by Alister Mackenzie (1925); by H. S. Colt and C. H. Alison (remodeled 9, 1930), and J.J.F. Penninck (1975).

ROYAL MELBOURNE GOLF CLUB

Melbourne, Australia, Composite Course, 18/6,946/72

Alister Mackenzie and Alex Russell (1926). Remodeled by Dick Wilson (1959).

ROYAL PORTRUSH GOLF CLUB

Portrush, Northern Ireland, Dunluce Course, 18/6,810/73

H. S. Colt (1920). Remodeled by J.S.F. Morrison (1946).

ROYAL TROON GOLF CLUB

Troon, Scotland, Old Course, 18/7,067/72

Charles Hunter (1878). Remodeled by Willie Fernie (1900), James Braid (1923), Alister Mackenzie (1907), and J.S.F. Morrison (1957).

ST. ANDREWS

Fife, Scotland, Old Course, 18/6,950/72

Sixteenth century. Remodeled by Allan Robertson (1848), Old Tom Morris, Alister Mackenzie, James Braid, and John R. Stutt.

SAN FRANCISCO GOLF CLUB

San Francisco, California, U.S.A., 18/6,623/71

A.W. Tillinghast (1918). Remodeled by William P. Bell (1947).

SEMINOLE GOLF CLUB

North Palm Beach, Florida, U.S.A., 18/6,752/72

Donald Ross (1929). Remodeled by Dick Wilson (1947) and Ed Connor (1991).

SHINNECOCK HILLS GOLF CLUB

Southampton, New York, U.S.A., 18/6,697/72

William S. Flynn and Howard Toomey (1931). Remodeled by William F. Mitchell (1967).

SOUTHERN HILLS COUNTRY CLUB

Tulsa, Oklahoma, U.S.A., 18/7,037/71

Perry Maxwell (1935). Remodeled by Robert Trent Jones (1957), George and Tom Fazio (1976), an by Bill Coore and Ben Crenshaw (additional 9, 1992).

SUNNINGDALE GOLF CLUB
Berkshire, England, Old Course 18/6,533/72

Willie Park, Jr.(1901). Remodeled by H. S. Colt and C. H. Alison (1922), C. K. Cotton, and D.M.A. Steel (1986).

TURNBERRY GOLF CLUB
Turnberry, Strathclyde, Scotland, Ailsa Course, 18/7,060/71

Willie Fernie (1909). Remodeled by C. K. Hutchinson (1938), P. M. Ross and James Alexander (1951), and Peter Alliss and David Thomas (1976).

WINGED FOOT GOLF CLUB
Mamaroneck, New York, U.S.A., West Course, 18/6,956/72

A.W. Tillinghast (1923). Remodeled by Robert Trent Jones (1958), Dick Wilson (1958), George and Tom Fazio (1973), and Tom Fazio (1989).

WOODHALL SPA GOLF CLUB
Woodhall Spa, England, 18/6,866/73

Harry Vardon (1905). Remodeled by H. S. Colt (1912), S. V. Hotchkin (1922), Sir Guy Campbell, C. K. Hutchinson, and S. V. Hotchkin (1926).

THE PEOPLE'S 300 PLUS COURSES

Below are more than three hundred courses in North America, Bermuda, the Bahamas, and the Caribbean that you can play. Consult the travel section of this book for tour and discount sources.

United States

ALABAMA

GRAND NATIONAL GOLF CLUB
(54, PUBLIC)
Opelika
(205) 749-9042
(800) 949-4444

One stop on the Robert Trent Jones, Sr., Trail of Golf; inquire about other courses on the trail, all within the state. One of golf's best bargains. Venues: Lake Course, Links Course, and Short Course.

MARRIOTT'S LAKE-WOOD GOLF CLUB
(36, RESORT)
Point Clear
(205) 990-6312
(800) 544-9933

Situated on a peninsula jutting into Mobile Bay. *Azalea*: well treed, requires accuracy and shot management. *Dogwood*: Also well treed with large greens protected by clusters of bunkers.

ALASKA

EAGLEGLEN GOLF COURSE
(18, PUBLIC)
6,024 yards/par 72
Anchorage
(907) 552-3821

Robert Trent Jones, Sr., layout with sixty-five bunkers, large well-guarded greens, variety of hole layouts, distances, and doglegs.

ARIZONA

THE BOULDERS
(36, RESORT)
Carefree
(602) 488-9009
(800) 553-1717

Beautiful desert layouts with rolling fairways, well-placed fairway bunkers, large undulating greens protected with an array of bunkers. New practice area.

LOEWS VENTANA
CANYON RESORT
(36, RESORT)
Tucson
(520) 299-2020
(800) 235-6397

Two Tom Fazio layouts on 1,100 acres backed by the Santa Catalina Mountains. Canyon and Mountain Courses are hilly, bordered by desert with a variety of well-trapped greens, some multitiered, forced carries over desert.

LOS CABALLEROS
GOLF CLUB
(18, RESORT)
6,577 yards/par 72
Wickenburg
(602) 684-2704

A hidden gem in dude-ranch country where gold was once the craze. Lush fairways, medium-sized tricky greens often fronted by bunkers; wind can be a factor.

SEDONA GOLF RESORT
(18, RESORT)
6,126 yards/par 71
Oak Creek
(602) 284-9355

Excellent Gary Panks-designed layout surrounded by the magnificent towering pinnacles and sheer red sandstone canyon walls of the red-rock country of Sedona. Elevation changes, large undulating bentgrass greens protected by traps.

TOURNAMENT
PLAYERS CLUB OF
SCOTTSDALE
(36, PUBLIC)
Scottsdale
(602) 585-3935
(800) 223-1818

Jay Morrish and Tom Weiskopf-designed layouts including the Stadium Course, site of the Phoenix Open. Stadium features knolls, spectator mounds, a variety of well-protected greens, and desert winds; water comes into play on six holes on the back nine.

STAR PASS GOLF CLUB
(18, PUBLIC)
6,383 yards/Par 72
Tucson
(520) 670-0300

Rolling fairways bordered by cactus, wildflowers, sagebrush, and other desert foliage; demands shotmaking skill. Site of PGA Northern Telecom Open; designed by Robert Cupp.

TROON NORTH
(18, PUBLIC)
6,474 yards/par 72
Scottsdale
(602) 585-7700

Weiskopf and Morrish-designed golf adventure through arroyos, natural washes, saguaro cactus, and other spectacular desert vegetation.

With the advance of golf training and technology, records seem to fall on a regular basis. It is not uncommon for 72-hole PGA tournaments to be won with scores of 20-under-par or better. Unless a course can be lengthened or unless it is toughened up with lightning-fast greens and high rough, it is likely that someone will rain down on the course with birdies. Yet there are some venerable records that remain and will be hard to surpass.

• One of these is Mike Souchak's 72-hole total of 257 (60-68-64-65) recorded in the 1955 Texas Open at Brackenridge Park in San Antonio. Souchak's record 27 on the second nine of the first round in the same event stood for twenty years until Andy North tied it at the B.C. Open at the En-Joie Golf Club.

• Byron Nelson still holds the record for most consecutive victories (eleven) and most wins in one year (eighteen), which he set during 1945.

• Sam Snead holds the career record for PGA-Tour-cosponsored and/or -approved tournaments with eighty-one.

• Walter Hagen holds the record for most consecutive victories in a single event. Walter won four straight PGA Championships beginning in 1924.

• Sam Snead holds the non-adjusted Vardon Trophy best-scoring average with 69.23 strokes per round in 96 rounds in 1950. Greg Norman holds the modern record with 68.81 set in 1994.

**TUCSON NATIONAL
(27, RESORT)**
Tucson
(520) 297-2271
(800) 528-4856

No forced carries over desert, but a variety of water hazards and strategically placed fairway bunkers; well-trapped bentgrass greens. Hilly in spots with wind a factor.

**THE WESTIN LA PALOMA RESORT
(27, RESORT)**
Tucson
(602) 742-6000
(800) 222-1252

Nicklaus-designed natural-desert target golf course with no water, within 790-acre planned community. Ridge/Canyon combination has 142 slope and 75 rating from the back tees.

**THE WIGWAM RESORT
(54, RESORT)**
Litchfield Park
(602) 935-3811
(800) 327-0396

Three excellent venues, the Gold and Blue Courses designed by Robert Trent Jones, Sr., and the West by Red Lawrence, in recently restored resort dating back to 1918.

ARKANSAS

**MOUNTAIN RANCH GOLF COURSE
(18, RESORT)**
6,280 yards/par 72
Fairfield Bay
(501) 884-6092

Edmund Ault-designed, rolling hilly layout within real estate development. Front nine open, back nine tightly treed, with large greens; well bunkered; dramatic elevation changes.

CALIFORNIA

**LA COSTA RESORT AND SPA
(36, RESORT)**
Carlsbad
(619) 438-9111
(800) 854-5000

Dick Wilson and Joe Lee layouts in a 100-acre luxury real estate development. North Course, site of PGA Infiniti Tournament of Champions, has water on seven holes, rolling terrain, and well trapped greens. Wind a factor, especially on South Course, a quality venue.

**LA QUINTA HOTEL, GOLF AND TENNIS RESORT
(36, RESORT)**
La Quinta
(619) 564-4111
(800) 472-4316 (CA)
(800) 854-1271 (outside CA)

Pete Dye-designed Dunes and Citrus Courses. Dunes, a target course with water on seven holes, well-guarded greens. Citrus is also a target course with water on five holes.

**THE LINKS AT SPANISH BAY
(18, RESORT)**
6,078 yards/par 72
Pebble Beach
(408) 647-7500
(800) 654-9300

Situated among Scottish-style dunes bordering the Pacific. Variety of doglegs, well bunkered, large undulating greens, wind a factor. Sloped at 133 from the middle tees.

**OJAI VALLEY INN AND COUNTRY CLUB
(18, RESORT)**
6,252 yards/par 70
Ojai
(805) 646-5511
(800) 422-6524

A traditional course on rolling former ranchland, mature trees, well-trapped bentgrass greens, doglegs, dramatic elevation changes. A gem backed by the Topa Topu Mountains.

**PASATIEMPO
(18, PUBLIC)**
6,154 yards/par 71
Santa Cruz
(408) 426-3622

Hilly traditional layout designed by Alister Mackenzie (1929) within an early golf real estate community. The first foursome to tee off included Bobby Jones and Glenna Collett Vare, winner of six U.S. Women's Amateurs. The 1986 U.S. Womens's Amateur was held here.

**PEBBLE BEACH
GOLF LINKS
(18, RESORT)**
6,357 yards/par 72
Pebble Beach
(408) 624-3811
(800) 654-9300

One of the best in the world; eight holes directly on the Pacific, with wind a factor. A strategic golf course with a variety of holes ranging from the 107-yard par-3 seventh toward the ocean to the 565-yard par-5 fourteenth which runs inland.

**PELICAN HILL GOLF
CLUB
(36, RESORT)**
6,312 yards/par 70
Newport Coast
(714) 760-0707

Tom Fazio-designed layouts in the hills overlooking the Pacific. Elevation changes, tricky large greens; strategic shotmaking and course management a must.

**PGA WEST—
JACK NICKLAUS
RESORT COURSE
(18, RESORT)**
6,546 yards/par 72
La Quinta
(619) 564-7170

Jack Nicklaus design, water on seven holes, large undulating bentgrass greens; positioning off the tee and accuracy extremely important.

**PGA WEST
—TPC STADIUM
COURSE
(18, RESORT)**
6,753 yards/par 72
La Quinta
(619) 564-7170

Famous Pete Dye creation, sloped at 151 and rated 77.3 from the back tees. Undulating fairways, deep bunkers, water on half the holes, elevation changes, large undulating bentgrass greens. Pick the right tee distance—five to choose from.

**POPPY HILLS
(18, PUBLIC)**
6,288 yards/Par 72
Pebble Beach
(408) 625-2035

Robert Trent Jones, Jr.-designed layout with rolling fairways, ocean winds, large well-bunkered greens. Home of the Northern California Golf Association and site of the PGA AT&T Pebble Beach event.

**SILVERADO
COUNTRY CLUB
(36, RESORT)**
Napa
(707) 257-0200
(800) 532-0500

Traditional early Robert Trent Jones, Jr., design with mature trees and rolling layouts in wine country. Site of PGA Senior Tour Transamerica event.

SPYGLASS HILL GOLF COURSE (18, RESORT)
6,277 yards/par 72
Pebble Beach
(408) 649-2711
(800) 654-9300

Robert Trent Jones, Sr., described his layout this way: "The first five holes were designed with Pine Valley in mind, and the remainder are designed like Augusta National, with its majestic pines, lofty ocean views, challenging bunkers protecting landing areas, lakes to grab the errant shot, well-bunkered greens and a challenging putting surface."

TORREY PINES GOLF COURSE (36, PUBLIC)
La Jolla
(619) 453-0380

Two excellent William F. Bell municipal courses overlooking the Pacific. Open, windswept, pine and eucalyptus trees, medium-sized bentgrass greens, strategically placed bunkers. Hosts PGA Buick Invitational of California.

COLORADO

THE BROADMOOR GOLF CLUB (54, RESORT)
Colorado Springs
(719) 577-5775
(800) 634-7111

Fifty-four holes of classic Donald Ross, Robert Trent Jones, Sr., and Arnold Palmer/Ed Seay mountain golf. Jack Nicklaus won the U.S. Amateur here in 1959. A Colorado golf shrine and five-star resort.

KEYSTONE RANCH (18, RESORT)
6,521 yards/par 72
Keystone
(303) 468-4250
(800) 222-0188

Situated at 9,300 feet in the Rockies. First four carved out of woods; gives way to open linksland style, then plays through a valley back to the clubhouse. Water hazards, varied magnificent terrain.

POLE CREEK GOLF CLUB (18, PUBLIC)
6,413 yards/par 72
Winter Park
(303) 726-8847

Cut through pine forests at 8,900 feet in the Rockies with wildlife such as elk and hawks in abundance. Shotmaker's course, elevation changes, water on eleven holes, medium-sized bentgrass greens.

RIVERDALE GOLF COURSE (36, PUBLIC)
Brighton
(303) 659-6700

Perry and Pete Dye-designed all-bentgrass Dunes Course features large landing areas, large undulating, difficult greens well guarded by water, traps, and grass-pot bunkers. Henry T. Hughes-designed Knolls Course is more forgiving.

SINGLETREE GOLF CLUB
(18, RESORT)
6,423 yards/par 71
Vail
(303) 476-5656
(800) 654-8312

Designed by Jack Nicklaus, Robert Cupp, and Jay Morrish. Front nine somewhat flat, back nine hilly. Generous landing areas, small bentgrass greens well guarded by traps and water. Bring your short game.

TAMARRON GOLF COURSE
(18, RESORT)
6,340 yards/par 72
Durango
(303) 259-2000
(800) 678-1000

Arthur Hills layout cut through oak, aspen, and ponderosa pine at 7,600 feet in the San Juan Mountains. Tight fairways; large fast, undulating greens protected by large bunkers; elevation changes; water hazards—a difficult test of golf.

CONNECTICUT

RICHTER PARK
(18, PUBLIC)
6,307 yards/par 72
Danbury
(203) 792-2552

Wooded, hilly, park setting, large well-trapped greens, water hazards on a majority of the holes. Very popular venue.

FLORIDA

Amelia Island Plantation
(45, Resort)
Amelia Island
(904) 261-6161
(800) 342-6841 (FL)
(800) 874-6878
    (outside FL)
Pete Dye-designed Amelia Links is short, tight, well treed, with winds through wetlands, some ocean holes. Long Point, designed by Tom Fazio, is a more open layout with wooded terrain, water, and some ocean holes.

ARNOLD PALMER'S BAY HILL CLUB AND LODGE
(27, RESORT)
Orlando
(407) 876-2429
(800) 523-5999

Arnold Palmer's course and site of the PGA Tour Nestle Invitational. Challenger/Champion best venue with rolling fairways, doglegs, large well-guarded greens.

DORAL RESORT AND COUNTRY CLUB
(90, RESORT)
Miami
(305) 592-2000
(800) 327-6334

Major resort with all the amenities. Blue Course, designed by Rick Wilson and Robert von Hagge, hosts the Doral Ryder Open.

EASTWOOD GOLF COURSE
(18, PUBLIC)
6,234 yards/par 72
Fort Myers
(813) 275-4848

Heavily played quality Devlin and von Hagge layout, rolling terrain, water hazards on more than half the holes. Front nine tightly treed, back nine has over eighty bunkers.

**GATEWAY GOLF
AND COUNTRY CLUB
(18, SEMIPRIVATE)**
6,606 yards/par 72
Fort Myers
(813) 561-1010

Tom Fazio design with
more than ninety bunkers,
abundant water hazards,
large well-guarded greens,
windswept.

**GRAND CYPRESS
RESORT
(45, RESORT)**
Orlando
(407) 239-4700
(800) 835-7377

Jack Nicklaus-designed
traditional (twenty-seven
holes) and links-style layouts; three specially
designed practice holes.
Top-of-the-line resort.

**GRENELEFE RESORT
AND CONFERENCE
CENTER
(54, RESORT)**
Haines City
(813) 422-7511
(800) 282-7875 (FL)
(800) 237-9549
   (outside FL)

Rolling fairways bordered
by pine and oak. The West
Course, designed by
Robert Trent Jones, Sr.,
with its length (7,325 yards
from the back tees), tight
fairways, and well-pro-
tected greens, will test your
golf game.

**INNISBROOK
HILTON RESORT
(63, RESORT)**
Palm Harbor
(813) 942-2000
(800) 456-2000

Copperhead layout with
seventy-three traps, ten
water hazards, undulating
greens winding through
pines; site of J. C. Penney
Classic. Sandpiper (twenty-
seven holes) and Island
(eighteen) are excellent
venues.

**LELY FLAMINGO
ISLAND CLUB
(18, RESORT)**
6,527 yards/par 72
Naples
(813) 793-2223

Robert Trent Jones, Sr.,
layout within planned community. Rolling fairways,
palmetto and cypress trees,
large greens, water on thirteen holes, well bunkered,
winds from the Gulf of
Mexico.

**LINKS AT KEY
BISCAYNE
(18, PUBLIC)**
6,389 yards/par 72
Key Biscayne
(305) 361-9139

Varied von Hagge and
Devlin layout with water
on thirteen holes, medium-
to-large well-bunkered
greens; near the Bay,
windswept. A Senior Tour
stop.

**MARRIOTT'S BAY
POINT RESORT
(36, RESORT)**
Panama City
(904) 234-3307
(800) 874-7105

Lagoon legend, designed
by Devlin and von Hagge,
has highest slope rating
(152) in Florida. Water
hazards on almost every
hole, well bunkered, winds
off Gulf of Mexico. Club
Meadows Course tight,
small greens, windswept.

MARRIOTT'S MARCO ISLAND RESORT AND GOLF CLUB (18, RESORT)
6,471 yards/par 72
Marco Island
(813) 394-2511
(800) 438-4373

Joe Lee design cut through Australian pine and palm, seventy-four traps and water hazards on fifteen holes, well-trapped greens, wind a factor.

MARRIOTT'S SAWGRASS RESORT (99, RESORT)
Ponte Vedra
(904) 285-7777
(800) 457-4653

Home of Pete Dye's TPC Stadium Course with famous island-green seventeenth, other excellent courses.

PELICAN'S NEST GOLF CLUB (36, RESORT)
Bonita Springs
(813) 947-4600
(800) 952-6378

Tom Fazio-designed layouts within real estate community. Shot placement and course management a must to cope with palmettos, wind, water hazards, strategically placed bunkers.

THE NINETEENTH HOLE

After a round it might be fittng to have another round at the 19th hole. Some golf cocktails from *The Mr. Boston Deluxe Official Bartenders Guide*, published by the Mr. Boston Distiller Corporation in Boston:

Country Club Cooler
1/2 teaspoon of Grenadine, 2 oz. carbonated water in collins glass and stir. Add ice cubes and 2 oz. dry Vermouth. fill with carbonated water or ginger ale and stir again. Insert spiral of orange or lemon peel and dangle end over rim of glass.

Golf Cocktail
1 1/2 oz. of dry gin, 3/4 oz. dry Vermouth, 2 dashes of bitters; stir with ice and strain into a cocktail glass.

Hole-in-One Cocktail
3/4 oz. dry Vermouth, 1 1/2 oz. dry gin, 2 dashes of orange bitters, stir with ice, strain into a cocktail glass, and add an olive.

PGA NATIONAL GOLF CLUB
(90, RESORT)
Palm Beach Gardens
(407) 627-2000

PGA headquarters, full resort with excellent golf facilities. The Champion, with five tee positions ranging from 5,645 to 7,022 yards, is the best layout and the site of the PGA Seniors.

THE WALT DISNEY WORLD RESORT
(99, RESORT)
Lake Buena Vista
(407) 824-2270

Excellent venues (plus a nine-hole executive course) within Walt Disney World. Designed by Joe Lee, Tom Fazio, and Pete Dye. A great place for a golf gourmand.

WEST PALM BEACH COUNTRY CLUB
(18, PUBLIC)
6,523 yards/par 72
West Palm Beach
(407) 582-2019

Windswept Dick Wilson design on dunes; no water hazards, many traps, well treed, on two hundred acres of land.

WORLD WOODS GOLF CLUB
(45, PUBLIC)
Brooksville
(904) 796-5500

Excellent new facility sixty-five miles south of Tampa. Pine Barrens a tough layout with waste bunkers, elevation changes, penal. Rolling Oaks more user-friendly. Nine-hole executive course plus superb practice facility.

GEORGIA

CALLAWAY GARDENS
(63, RESORT)
Pine Mountain
(706) 663-2281
(800) 282-8181

Mountain View Course is the site of the PGA Tour's Buick Southern Open. Resort consisting of twelve thousand acres situated among woodlands, lakes, gardens, and abundant wildlife.

JONES CREEK GOLF CLUB
(18, PUBLIC)
6,557 yards/par 72
Evans
(706) 860-4228

Rees Jones design within 520-acre planned community five minutes from Augusta National. Woodlands, winding creeks, rolling terrain, large undulating bentgrass greens, well bunkered, water hazards on eight holes.

LAKE LANIER HILTON RESORT
(18, RESORT)
6,104 yards/par 72
Lake Lanier Islands
(404) 945-8787
(800) 768-5253

Joe Lee-designed layout includes thirteen holes bordering Lake Lanier, seventy-five bunkers, large undulat-ing greens, tight rolling fairways.

OSPREY COVE
(18, PUBLIC)
6,269 yards/par 72
St. Mary's
(912) 882-5575
(800) 352-5575

Mark McCumber design rolls through wetlands and woodlands. Generous landing areas and distances from green to next hole. Large undulating bentgrass greens well protected by bunkers.

**PORT ARMOR
(18, RESORT)**
6,285 yards/par 72
Greensboro
(706) 453-4564

Robert Cupp layout within
six hundred-acre real estate
development on Lake
Okonee. Rolling fairways,
dramatic elevation changes,
bunkers, mounds or water
guards medium-sized
undulating greens.

**REYNOLDS
PLANTATION CLUB
(36, RESORT)**
Greensboro
(706) 467-3159

The Plantation Course is a
tree-lined Robert Cupp
design with tough greens,
rated one of the best golf
courses in Georgia. The
new Nicklaus-designed
Great Waters layout is a
must play with water on
nine of the last ten holes.

**THE SEA ISLAND
GOLF CLUB
(36, RESORT)**
St. Simons Island
(912) 638-3611
(800) 732-4752

Travis, Colt, and Alison
nines of the 1920s, recently
renovated by Rees Jones.
Also Joe Lee and Dick
Wilson nines that can be
played in combination with
older layouts at five-star
resort. Nearby is another
eighteen holes at the St.
Simons Island Club.

**SOUTHBRIDGE
GOLF CLUB
(18, SEMIPRIVATE)**
6,458 yards/par 72
Savannah
(912) 651-5455
(800) 852-4255
   (outside GA)

Mounded rolling fairways
cut through oak, pine, and
dogwood. Mixture of
doglegs and large undulating greens; water hazards
on more than half the
holes.

**STONE MOUNTAIN
PARK GOLF COURSE
(36, RESORT)**
Stone Mountain
(404) 498-5715
(800) 879-9900

Rolling, tight, scenic well-
bunkered layouts cut
through forest in 3,200-
acre Stone Mountain State
Park, home of The Con-
federate Memorial, the
world's largest sculpture.

HAWAII

**KAPALUA GOLF CLUB
(54, RESORT)**
Lahaina, Maui
(808) 669-8044
(800) 367-8000

Bill Coore and Ben Cren-
shaw Plantation Course on
former pineapple planta-
tion. Large undulating
well-trapped greens, dra-
matic elevation changes,
ocean and mountain vistas.
Also two Arnold Palmer
courses.

**KAUAI LAGOONS
RESORT
(36, RESORT)**
Lihue, Kauai
(808) 246-5061
(800) 634-6400

Jack Nicklaus layouts
include Kiele, perched
along the Pacific and featuring undulating greens,
numerous bunkers, rolling
hills, deep ravines, natural
vegetation, water hazards
on eight holes, and trade
winds. The Lagoon Course
is more forgiving.

**KO OLINA GOLF CLUB
(18, RESORT)**
6,324 yards/par 72
Ewa Beach, Oahu
(808) 676-5300
(800) 626-4447

Ted Robinson oceanside design has rolling fairways, medium-sized undulating greens, water hazards on half the holes, tough Bermuda rough, bunkers guarding landing areas and greens. Wind a factor.

**THE KING'S GOLF CLUB
(18, RESORT)**
6,584 yards/par 72
Waikoloa, Hawaii
(808) 885-4647

Tom Weiskopf and Jay Morrish design with ninety-five bunkers, six water hazards, well-guarded large, varied greens.

**MAUNA KEA GOLF
COURSE
(18, RESORT)**
6,737 yards/Par 72
Kohala Coast, Hawaii
(808) 882-7222
(800) 882-6060

Robert Trent Jones, Sr., design carved from lava rock; dramatic seaside elevation changes, large well-bunkered greens, wind a factor.

**MAUNA LANI RESORT
(36, RESORT)**
Kohala Coast, Hawaii
(808) 885-6622
(800) 367-2323

North Course at seaside resort has rolling terrain, mesquite forests, well-trapped large greens, elevation changes, kona winds. Senior Skins Game is held on the South Course.

**PRINCEVILLE RESORT
(45, RESORT)**
Princeville, Kauai
(808) 826-3580
(800) 826-4400

Robert Trent Jones, Jr., designs featuring the Prince Course, a steep and narrow layout bordering the Pacific. Deep ravines, tropical jungles, streams, waterfalls, uneven lies, fast undulating greens, tricky winds, grass and sand bunkering. Five tee distances. Also the twenty-seven-hole Makai Course.

IDAHO

**COEUR D'ALENE
(18, RESORT)**
6,309 yards/par 71
Coeur d'Alene
(208) 667-4653
(800) 841-5868 (ID)
(800) 688-5253
   (outside ID)

On Lake Coeur d'Alene, bentgrass throughout, famous computerized floating par-3 green, well-trapped greens.

**SUN VALLEY RESORT
GOLF COURSE
(18, RESORT)**
6,057 yards/par 72
Sun Valley
(208) 622-2251
(800) 786-8259

Shotmaker's course on rolling terrain, well treed, well bunkered, water on thirteen holes, large bentgrass greens.

ILLINOIS

**ANNBRIAR GOLF
COURSE
(18, PUBLIC)**
6,407 yards/par 72
Waterloo
(618) 939-4653

Designed by Michael Hurdzan, front nine open, back nine wooded with elevation changes, abundant water hazards, large greens, 114 bunkers. Sloped at 141 from back tees (6,841 yards).

CANTIGNY GOLF COURSE
(27, PUBLIC)
Wheaton
(708) 668-3323

Beautifully maintained Packard-designed layouts on the McCormick estate. Well treed, bentgrass throughout, water hazards on twelve holes, strategically bunkered medium-sized greens.

COG HILL GOLF AND COUNTRY CLUB
(72, PUBLIC)
Lemont
(708) 257-5872

Dick Wilson- and Joe Lee-designed Cog Hill No. 4 is the site of the Western Open. Excellent public golf facility with quality practice amenities.

EAGLE RIDGE INN AND RESORT
(45, RESORT)
Galena
(815) 777-2500
(800) 892-2269

Roger Packard-designed scenic layouts within 6,800-acre real estate development. North Course features dramatic elevation changes; well treed, large well-protected greens, water on seven of back nine holes. South and nine-hole executive courses.

KEMPER LAKES GOLF CLUB
(18, PUBLIC)
6,680 yards/par 72
Long Grove
(708) 540-3450

Ken Killian and Dick Nugent design featuring 125 acres of lakes, rolling terrain, large undulating bentgrass greens protected by traps and water hazards. Site of 1989 PGA Championship and other national events.

PINE MEADOW GOLF CLUB
(18, PUBLIC)
6,614 yards/par 72
Mundelein
(708) 566-4653

Joe Lee and Rocky Roquemore venue converted from an arboreteum. Beautifully treed hilly terrain with bentgrass throughout; large undulating greens well protected by huge sand traps. Lakes and ponds come into play on six holes.

SPENCER T. OLIN COMMUNITY GOLF COURSE
(18, PUBLIC)
6,414 yards/par 72
Alton
(618) 465-3111

Palmer-designed layout, hilly, well treed, with large undulating greens protected by sizeable bunkers; water comes into play on half the holes.

INDIANA

BRICKYARD CROSSING
(18, PUBLIC)
6,621 yards/par 72
Indianapolis
(317) 484-6572

Brickyard Crossing is a complete Pete Dye remake of The Speedway Golf Course which hosted the 500 Festival Open, a P.G.A. tour event until 1968. More than 1.5 million cubic yards of earth were moved to create sculpted rolling fairways, knolls, viewing mounds and the large undulating bentgrass greens on this layout. Little Eagle Creek runs through the golf course, coming into play on eight holes and three lakes affect play on three other holes. Four holes are located within the center of the renowned Speedway Oval, a splendid spot from which to tee it up.

GOLF CLUB OF INDIANA
(18, PUBLIC)
6,438 yards/par 72
Lebanon
(317) 769-6388

Rolling open farmland, more than seventy-five bunkers, water hazards on fifteen holes, large undulating bentgrass greens guarded by sand and water.

HULMAN LINKS
GOLF COURSE
(18, PUBLIC)
6,740 yards/par 72
Terre Haute
(812) 877-2096

Tough course on 230 acres of rolling hills. Doglegs, elevation changes, blind shots, large well-bunkered bentgrass greens, well-guarded landing areas, uneven lies. Sloped at 144 from back tees (7,225 yards) and 134 from forward tees (5,775 yards).

OTTER CREEK
GOLF COURSE
(18, PUBLIC)
6,557 yards/par 72
Columbus
(812) 579-5227

Country club-quality layout on 218 acres of well-treed rolling land. Completely bentgrass, blue grass rough; ninety bunkers, large tiered or undulating well-bunkered greens. A Robert Trent Jones, Sr., design.

IOWA

AMANA COLONIES
GOLF COURSE
(18, PUBLIC)
6,468 yards/par 72
Amana
(319) 622-6222
(800) 383-3636

Rolling fairways cut through dense hardwood forests, tight, variety of elevation changes, large undulating greens well protected by traps, uneven lies, bentgrass throughout, five tee distances.

KANSAS

DEER CREEK
GOLF CLUB
(18, SEMIPRIVATE)
6,368 yards/par 72
Overland Park
(913) 681-3100

Robert Trent Jones, Jr., layout, an original Hogan Tour site. Tight well-treed fairways, eighty-five bunkers, thirteen water holes, pronounced elevation changes, large well-protected bentgrass greens.

KENTUCKY

KEARNEY HILL
GOLF LINKS
(18, PUBLIC)
6,501 yards/par 72
Lexington
(606) 253-1981

Pete and Perry Dye layout
on rolling terrain with
large undulating, well-
trapped greens.

LOUISIANA

THE BLUFFS ON
THOMPSON CREEK
(18, RESORT)
6,533 yards/par 72
St. Francisville
(504) 634-5222

Situated in 534-acre real
estate development in an
area where John James
Audubon painted "Birds of
America." Palmer, Seay,
and Minchew design
carved through pine and
hardwood forests; dramatic
elevation changes, well
bunkered, with water haz-
ards on almost every hole,
large fast greens. Sloped at
142 from the back tees.

MAINE

SABLE OAKS
GOLF CLUB
(18, PUBLIC)
6,056 yards/par 72
South Portland
(207) 775-6257

Rolling, tightly treed;
water hazards on half the
holes; blind shots.
Designed by Geoffrey Cor-
nish and Brian Silva.

SAMOSET RESORT
GOLF CLUB
(18, RESORT)
6,010 yards/par 72
Rockport
(207) 594-2511

Scenic, windswept ocean-
side course, large greens.

SUGARLOAF
GOLF CLUB
(18, RESORT)
6,400 yards/par 72
Carrabassett Valley
 (207) 237-2000
(800) 843-5623

Robert Trent Jones, Jr.,
design, tight, well treed,
dramatic elevation changes;
accuracy and proper club
selection essential.

MARYLAND

EAGLE'S LANDING
GOLF COURSE
(18, PUBLIC)
6,300 yards/par 72
Berlin
(410) 213-7277
(800) 283-3846

Links-style course in scenic
wetlands, large bentgrass
greens, water hazards on
sixteen holes.

HOG NECK GOLF
COURSE
(18, PUBLIC)
5,922 yards/par 72
Easton
(410) 822-6079

Front nine open, windy,
with strategic sand traps
and water hazards; back
nine tightly treed. Has
nine-hole executive course.

QUEENSTOWN
HARBOR GOLF LINKS
(36, PUBLIC)
Queenstown
(410) 827-6611
(800) 827-5257

Beautifully situated along the Chesapeake, winding through woods with water hazards on most holes. Course management, accuracy a must. River/Woods the preferred venue.

MASSACHUSETTS

THE CAPTAIN'S GOLF COURSE
(18, PUBLIC)
6,176 yards/par 72
Brewster
(508) 896-5100

Flat, treelined, medium-sized, large, fast greens; wind; accuracy required. Designed by Cornish and Silva.

CRUMPIN-FOX CLUB
(18, PUBLIC)
6,508 yards/par 72
Bernardston
(413) 648-9101

Well treed, hilly, large well-trapped greens, water hazards on half the holes. Roger Rulewich and Robert Trent Jones, Sr., beauty.

NEW SEABURY RESORT AND CONFERENCE CENTER
(36, RESORT)
New Seabury
(508) 477-9111
(800) 752-9700 (MA)
(800) 222-2044
　(outside MA)

Blue Course: Rolling, windswept, with water hazards on half the holes; large well-treed greens; well-treed back nine. *Green Course*: Shorter good walking course. Designed by William Mitchell.

TACONIC GOLF CLUB
(18, SEMIPRIVATE)
6,575 yards/par 71
Williamstown
(413) 458-3997

Rolling New England mountain golf, site of 1996 U.S. Senior Amateur, on Williams College campus.

MICHIGAN

BOYNE HIGHLANDS RESORT
(54, RESORT)
Harbor Springs
(616) 526-2171
(800) 462-6963

Heather and moor layouts the combined, compatible efforts of Robert Trent Jones, Sr., and William Newcomb at year-round resort. Water hazards on half the holes, well-guarded bentgrass greens, rolling fairways. Also, Donald Ross Memorial with replica Ross holes.

BOYNE MOUNTAIN RESORT
(45, RESORT)
Boyne Falls
(616) 549-2441
(800) 462-6963

William Newcomb layouts in ski country. Alpine Course meanders down Boyne Mountain, well-treed well-guarded bentgrass greens, hilly uneven lies, seven water hazards. Monument Course also routed down mountain, plus a nine-hole executive course.

DUNMAGLAS GOLF COURSE
(18, PUBLIC)
6,427 yards/par 72
Charlevoix
(616) 547-1022

When you look southwest from the elevated first tee at Dunmaglas, a 370-yard par-4, you can see Lake Charlevoix and Lake Michigan beyond Then you descend over 100 feet to the treelined landing area below nd work your way through fairways lined with birch, maple, apple, pine and other varieties. Dunmaglas requires length and accuracy off the tee. The most difficult hole on the course is the 436-yard dogleg par-4 fouth which requires a 225-yard tee shot in order to have a view across wetlands to a well-bunkered green framed by pines. The back nine at Dunmaglas open up into meadowlands that have the feel of a links-style golf course.

**ELK RIDGE
GOLF COURSE
(18, PUBLIC)**
6,615 yards/par 72
Atlanta
(517) 785-2275
(800) 626-4355

Within 425 acres of scenic woodlands and wetlands, tightly treed, large undulating bentgrass greens; well bunkered, with forced carries, doglegs, and water hazards. Jerry Matthews design with a slope of 144 from the tips (7,033 yards); four tee distances.

**GRAND HAVEN GOLF
CLUB
(18, PUBLIC)**
6,179 yards/par 72
Grand Haven
(616) 842-4040

Cut through duneland pines, large well-trapped greens; shotmaking and accuracy required. A Bruce Mathews design.

**GRAND
TRAVERSE RESORT
(36, RESORT)**
At Grand Traverse
   Village (Acme)
(616) 938-1620
(800) 748-0303

Jack Nicklaus-designed Bear layout open, but tough from back tees; generous landing areas; well-protected large, undulating bentgrass greens; traps, mounds, and water hazards. Spruce Run, a Newcomb and Kay layout, more of a resort course.

**HIGH POINTE GOLF
CLUB
(18, PUBLIC)**
6,140 yards/par 71
Williamsburg
(616) 267-9900
(800) 753-7888

First Tom Doak effort, built on a cherry orchard; variety of open Scottish-inspired links-style holes and treelined fairways. Shotmaking and course management needed.

**THOROUGHBRED GOLF
CLUB**
(18, resort)
6,463 yards/par 72
Rothbury
(616) 893-GOLF

The Thoroughbred is a recent Arthur Hills-designed addition to the Double JJ, the largest adult dude ranch in the United States, located just north of Muskegon in rolling wooded countryside. Water hazards including a lake, ponds and cranberry bogs add character and difficulty to the memorable course which offers self-contained holes strung through pine, fruit trees and a variety of hardwoods. A shotmakers course, the Thoroughbred requires you to hit landing areas and accurately approach the bentgrass greens in order to score. The 58-yard par-5 finishing hold, a dogleg left that wraps around Carpenter Lake, provides a dramatic and difficult conclusion to a course you will want to play more than once.

**TREETOPS SYLVAN RESORT
(54, RESORT)**
Gaylord
(517) 732-6711
(800) 444-6711

Robert Trent Jones, Sr., course cut through woods; dramatic elevation changes, tightly treed, bentgrass greens protected by large sand traps; water hazards on six holes. Excellent Tom Fazio and Rick Smith layouts on site in ski region.

**SHANTY CREEK/SCHUSS MOUNTAIN RESORT
(54, RESORT)**
Bellaire
(616) 533-8621
(800) 678-4111

Features The Legend, a Palmer/Seay design, hilly, well treed; water hazards on five holes; large undulating bentgrass greens well protected by large bunkers. Thirty-six holes at Shanty Creek, eighteen at Schuss Mountain.

**TIMBER RIDGE GOLF CLUB
(18, PUBLIC)**
6,061 yards/par 72
East Lansing
(517) 339-8000
(800) 233-6669

Cut from a hilly tree nursery; large, undulating bentgrass greens protected by sizeable traps; water hazards on six holes. A beautiful adventure in the woods.

MINNESOTA

**EDINBURGH USA
(18, PUBLIC)**
6,335 yards/par 72
Brooklyn Park
(612) 424-7060

Built on 158 acres of woodland; bentgrass throughout, well-bunkered large greens, landing areas guarded by sand, water, and trees. Robert Trent Jones, Jr., design.

**THE PINES AT GRAND VIEW LODGE
(18, RESORT)**
6,431 yards/par 72
Nisswa
(218) 963-3146
(800) 432-3788

Joel Goldstrand design cut through central Minnesota woodlands. Well treed, tight; shotmaking and accuracy required on this beautiful gem.

MISSISSIPPI

**TIMBERTON GOLF CLUB
(18, PUBLIC)**
6,463 yards/par 72
Hattiesburg
(601) 584-4653

Mark McCumber layout; open, large well-trapped greens; over seven thousand yards from the tips.

MISSOURI

THE LODGE OF FOUR SEASONS
(45, RESORT)
Lake Ozark
(314) 365-8532
(800) 843-5253

Features hilly Robert Trent Jones, Sr., design carved out of woods; borders Lake of Ozarks; well-trapped large, undulating bentgrass greens, within 3,200-acre resort real estate development. Executive nine-hole course available.

MONTANA

EAGLE BEND GOLF CLUB
(18, PUBLIC)
6,237 yards/par 72
Big Fork
(406) 837-7302
(800) 255-5641

Centerpiece of real estate development on Flathead Lake. Rolling terrain, water on seven holes, undulating greens, well protected by traps and water.

NEBRASKA

WOODLAND HILLS GOLF COURSE
(18, PUBLIC)
6,245 yards/par 71
Eagle
(402) 475-4653

Rolling terrain, well treed, heavily bunkered, water on five holes, large greens.

NEVADA

DESERT INN HOTEL AND COUNTRY CLUB
(18, RESORT)
6,633 yards/Par 72
Las Vegas
(702) 733-4290
(800) 634-6906

Lawrence Hughes-designed layout on 136 parklike acres. Rolling fairways; large undulating greens protected by large bunkers; mature trees; water hazards on seven holes.

EDGEWOOD TAHOE GOLF COURSE
(18, PUBLIC)
6,960 yards/par 72
Stateline
(702) 588-3566

George Fazio-designed scenic layout on 250 acres at 6,200 feet overlooking Lake Tahoe. Strategically placed trees, eighty bunkers, large undulating bentgrass greens, water hazards on eleven holes, forced carries.

NEW HAMPSHIRE

THE BALSAMS RESORT
(27, RESORT)
Dixville Notch
(603) 255-3400
(800) 255-0800 (NH)
(800) 255-0600
    (outside NH)

Panorama: well treed, hilly, old-style Donald Ross layout; water hazards, small crowned greens, difficult-to-read mountainside putts, no fee to hotel guests. *Coashaukee*: nine-hole short course.

EASTMAN GOLF LINKS
(18, SEMIPRIVATE)
6,338 yards/par 71
Grantham
(603) 863-4500

Scenic, hilly, well-treed mountain links course; large well-trapped greens.

PORTSMOUTH COUNTRY CLUB
(18, SEMIPRIVATE)
6,609 yards/par 72
Greenland
(603) 436-9719

Open layout, swept by seaside winds; the only Robert Trent Jones, Sr., course in New Hampshire.

SHATTUCK INN GOLF COURSE
(18, PUBLIC)
6,077 yards/par 71
Jaffrey
(603) 532-4300

Tight target course in wildlife setting, sixteen holes with wetlands or water; accuracy and course management a must. Bring enough golf balls.

SKY MEADOW COUNTRY CLUB
(18, SEMIPRIVATE)
6,036 yards/par 72
Nashua
(603) 888-9000
William Amick modern strategic layout. Variety of sand bunkers and water hazards; rolling terrain, doglegs, well-guarded greens.

NEW JERSEY

CRYSTAL SPRINGS GOLF CLUB
(18, SEMIPRIVATE)
6,411 yards/par 72
Hamburg
(201) 827-1444

Von Hagge-designed, hilly, well-treed, well-bunkered layout built in a quarry setting; water hazards on six holes; medium-to-large-sized undulating greens.

HOMINY HILL GOLF COURSE
(18, PUBLIC)
6,470 yards/par 72
Colts Neck
(908) 462-9222

Rolling open Robert Trent Jones, Sr., layout with over one hundred bunkers, large undulating greens. Site of 1983 U.S. Amateur Public Links.

MARRIOTT'S SEAVIEW GOLF RESORT
(36, RESORT)
Absecon
(609) 652-1800
(800) 932-8000

Donald Ross-designed Bay Course open, with small greens and over one hundred traps; Pines Course well treed, well bunkered, tight.

NEW MEXICO

THE INN OF THE MOUNTAIN GODS
(18, RESORT)
6,416 yards/par 72
Mescalero
(505) 257-5141
(800) 545-9011

Ted Robinson-designed mountain course at 7,200 feet within Apache Indian Reservation. Pronounced elevation changes, wind, well-treed fairways, undulating bentgrass greens; shotmaker's layout.

PINON HILLS GOLF COURSE
(18, PUBLIC)
6,736 yards/par 72
Farmington
(505) 326-6066

Dramatic elevation changes, forced carries, large well-protected greens, high desert beauty. Designed by Ken Dye.

NEW YORK

BETHPAGE BLACK
(18, PUBLIC)
6,556 yards/pr 71
Farmingdale
(516) 249-0700

Old-style A. W. Tillinghast masterpiece built in 1930s, rolling wooded acreage. Walking required, no carts. Four other courses within the state park.

THE CONCORD RESORT HOTEL
(45, RESORT)
Kiamesha Lake
(914) 794-4000
(800) 431-3850

Rolling layouts with mature trees and strategically placed water hazards and bunkers; "The Monster," the most noteworthy course here.

GLEN OAK GOLF COURSE
(18, PUBLIC)
6,232 yards/par 72
East Amherst
(716) 688-5454

Flat large greens protected by large bunkers; mature trees; water hazards on thirteen holes. Robert Trent Jones, Sr., design.

LEATHERSTOCKING GOLF CLUB
(18, RESORT)
6,006 yards/par 72
Cooperstown
(607) 547-9931
(800) 348-6222

Devereaux Emmett 1920s design with small well-trapped greens; along Lake Otsego.

MONTAUK DOWNS STATE PARK
(18, PUBLIC)
6,289 yards/par 72
Montauk
(516) 668-1100

Open, rolling, windswept Robert Trent Jones, Sr./Rees Jones collaboration near the ocean on Long Island.

SEVEN OAKS GOLF COURSE
(18, PUBLIC)
6,423 yards/par 72
Hamilton
(315) 824-1432

Robert Trent Jones, Sr., layout with rolling fairways, large well-bunkered greens, mature trees, and water on twelve holes. On Colgate University campus.

SPOOK ROCK
(18, PUBLIC)
6,366 yards/par 72
Ramapo
(914) 357-6466

Frank Duane-designed, rolling, treelined parklike layout with interesting doglegs; strategically placed traps and water hazards.

THE SAGAMORE RESORT AND GOLF COURSE
(18, RESORT)
6,410 yards/par 70
Bolton Landing
(518) 644-9400
(800) 358-3585

Old-style Donald Ross course overlooking Lake George. Well treed, hilly, with small crowned greens protected by bunkers.

SARANAC INN GOLF AND COUNTRY CLUB
(18, PUBLIC)
6,453 yards/par 72
Saranac Inn
(518) 891-1402

Turn-of-the-century Seymour Dunn Adirondack course; hilly, open; strategic bunkers; excellent condition.

SARATOGA SPA GOLF COURSE
(27, PUBLIC)
Saratoga Springs
(518) 587-8804

Championship course on rolling wooded state parkland; separate nine-hole executive course.

NORTH CAROLINA

DUKE UNIVERSITY GOLF CLUB
(18, PUBLIC)
6,721 yards/par 72
Durham
(919) 684-2817

Robert Trent Jones, Sr., layout remodeled by his son Rees in 1994.

LINVILLE GOLF CLUB
(18, RESORT)
6,286 yards/par 72
Linville
(704) 733-4363

Scenic Donald Ross (1926) layout, a shotmaker's course in the Carolina mountains.

MARSH HARBOR GOLF LINKS
(18, PUBLIC)
6,000 yards/par 71
Calabash
(910) 579-3161,
(800) 552-2660

Shotmaker's course, water hazards or treelined on half the holes, well bunkered, variously shaped medium-sized undulating greens.

OYSTER BAY GOLF LINKS
(18, PUBLIC)
6,435 yards/par 70

Lush marshland course, water hazards on fifteen holes, lagoons, lakes, intracoastal waterway, wildlife-preserve atmosphere.

PINEHURST RESORT AND COUNTRY CLUB
(126, RESORT)
Pinehurst
(910) 295-6811

Medley of Donald Ross, Rees Jones, Ellis Maples, and George and Tom Fazio layouts. Pinehurst No. 2 (Ross) and No. 7 (Jones) are the places to start.

TALAMORE AT PINEHURST
(18, PUBLIC)
6,720 yards/par 71
Southern Pines
(910) 692-5884

Challenging Rees Jones layout etched through rolling woodlands.

TANGLEWOOD PARK
(36, PUBLIC)
Clemmons
(910) 766-5082

Designed by Robert Trent Jones, Sr., and situated in 1,152-acre park. Championship course is site of PGA Senior Tour Vantage Championship and was the site of the 1986 Amateur Public Links Championship.

NORTH DAKOTA

EDGEWOOD GOLF COURSE
(18, PUBLIC)
6,045 yards/par 71
Fargo
(701) 232-2824

Rolling fairways guarded by oaks, elms, other varieties; large bentgrass greens on 1920s course renovated in 1951 by Robert Bruce Harris.

OHIO

AVALON LAKES GOLF COURSE
(18, RESORT)
6,453 yards/par 71
Warren
(216) 856-8898

Early Pete Dye (with William Newcomb) effort. Small-to-medium-sized greens well guarded by traps; water hazards on eleven holes; somewhat flat.

BLUE ASH GOLF COURSE
(18, PUBLIC)
6,211 yards/par 72
Blue Ash
(513) 745-8577

Hilly, well treed, medium-sized undulating bentgrass greens. Mature trees, hills, gullies, blind shots, and doglegs put emphasis on strategy and shotmaking. Designed by Jack Kidwell and Mike Hurdzan.

EAGLESTICKS GOLF CLUB
(18, PUBLIC)
6,028 yards/par 70
Zanesville
(614) 454-4900
(800) 782-4493

Hurdzan-designed target layout on old horse farm. Features large, fast undulating bentgrass greens and over 130 strategically placed traps.

SHAKER RUN GOLF CLUB
(18, PUBLIC)
6,600 yards/par 72
Lebanon
(513) 727-0007

Arthur Hills design. Former private club, shotmaker's course. Tightly treed on eight holes, dramatic elevation changes, back nine wooded but more open, water on ten holes, medium-sized greens.

THE VINEYARD GOLF COURSE
(18, PUBLIC)
6,254 yards/par 71
Cincinnati
(513) 474-3007

Country-club-quality, hilly, well treed; undulating bentgrass greens guarded by sand traps and water. Kidwell and Hurdzan design.

OKLAHOMA

KARSTEN CREEK
(18, SEMI-PRIVATE)
6,597 yards/par 72
Stillwater
(405) 743-1658

With five tee distances to choose from, this Tom Fazio-designed layout provides a walkable challenge through 230 acres of rolling treelined land within a low density real estate development near Oklahoma State University. Though there are only forty bunkers on the course, the variable wind, water hazards, tricky rough and mature trees will help your score to soar if you stray the ball.

SHANGRI-LA GOLF RESORT
(36, RESORT)
Afton
(918) 257-4204
(800) 331-4060

Two layouts with tee distances from 7,012 to 4,571 yards. Try the Blue Course: lakeside setting, tight fairways, tricky greens.

LONG BALL

Jack Hamm, the owner of Englewood, Colorado's Longball Sports Inc., has recently been notified by the *Guinness Book of World Records* that his drive of 473 yards has been accepted as a record at altitude. On July 20, 1993, Hamm hit his non-wind-aided drive 458 yards in the air at a driving range south of Denver. The feat is recorded in the 1995 edition of the Guinness record book.

OREGON

EASTMORELAND GOLF COURSE
(18, PUBLIC)
6,142 yards/par 72
Portland
(503) 775-2900

Parklike traditional layout set on 160 acres, designed by Lt. Chandler Egan (1917). A pleasure to play.

PUMPKIN RIDGE GOLF CLUB
(18, PUBLIC)
6,490 yards/par 71
Cornelius
(503) 647-9977

Ghost Creek Course: Robert Cupp design, Nike Tour site, bentgrass throughout, water on nine holes, varied green size, wind, well trapped. Private eighteen-hole Witch Hollow Course on site.

SALISHAN GOLF LINKS
(18, RESORT)
6,246 yards/par 72
Glenedan Beach
(503) 764-3632
(800) 452-2300

Oceanfront layout that weaves through forest, steep slopes, elevated bentgrass greens on the front side, and windswept ocean linksland on the back.

SUNRIVER LODGE RESORT GOLF COURSE
(36, RESORT)
Sunriver
(503) 593-1221
(800) 452-6874 (OR)
(800) 547-3922
    (outside OR)

Golf course real estate development. *South Course*: open meadowlands; long, windswept, water hazards; well-bunkered greens. *North*: tight, doglegs, greens well guarded by bunkers and water.

TOKATEE GOLF COURSE
(18, PUBLIC)
6,245 yards/par 72
Blue River
(503) 822-3220

Ted Robinson design with combination of meadowlands and forest, bentgrass greens well guarded by sand, fifteen lakes.

PENNSYLVANIA

CHAMPION LAKES GOLF CLUB
(18, PUBLIC)
6,205 yards/par 71
Bolivar
(412) 238-5440

Tightly-treed layout with strategically placed bunkers and water; high rough puts a premium on accuracy.

**HERSHEY
COUNTRY CLUB
(36, RESORT)**
Hershey
(717) 533-2171
(800) 437-7439

Maurice McCarthy-designed, well-bunkered West Course, site of the 1940 PGA championship. George Fazio-designed East Course also on rolling, open, wooded terrain.

**QUICKSILVER
GOLF CLUB
(18, PUBLIC)**
6,411 yards/par 72
Midway
(412) 796-1594/1811

Rolling, well-bunkered layout with large greens, difficult rough. Has been Nike and Senior Tour stop.

**TOFTREES RESORT
(18, RESORT)**
6,780 yards/par 72
State College
(814) 234-8000
(800) 458-3602
    (outside PA)

Edmund Ault-designed, rolling, well-treed layout within real estate development in Penn State country.

**WYNCOTE GOLF CLUB
(18, SEMI-PRIVATE)**
6,576 yards/par 72
Oxford

Wyncote is a links-style healthland gold course situated on open rolling farmland one hour southwest of Philadelphia just above the Maryland border. Etched in the midst of dairy, corn, soybean and other agricultural activity, Wyncote is a windswept shotmaker's layout with undulating bentgrass fairways, quick subtle greens, thick rough and more than seventy bunkers including 15 acres of waste bunkers. Wyncote offers a challenging variety of holes including the 577-yard par-5 opening holes, the 460-yard par-4 second and the 222-yard par-3 eighth, all of which often play into the wind. Mounds, bunkers and the occasional water hazard that protect Wyncote's immaculate greens, require accurate approach shots and a delicate touch with a widge should you miss the target.

RHODE ISLAND

**EXETER
COUNTRY CLUB
(18, SEMIPRIVATE)**
6,390 yards/par 72
Exeter
(401) 295-1178

Geoffrey Cornish-designed course with large well-bunkered greens, trees that come into play.

SOUTH CAROLINA

**HEATHER GLEN GOLF
LINKS (27, PUBLIC)**
North Myrtle Beach (803) 249-9000
(800) 868-4536

Scottish-style layout with numerous elevation changes; dogwood, oak, and other tree varieties; winding streams and brooks; heather-covered dunes, mounds.

**HERITAGE GOLF CLUB
(18, PUBLIC)**
6,575 yards/par 71
Pawleys Island
(803) 237-3424

Water comes into play on eight holes on this course; which features giant magnolias, oaks, crepe myrtle; camellias and azaleas; freshwater lakes and marshes; rice fields. Large undulating greens.

**KIAWAH
ISLAND RESORT
(72, RESORT)**
Kiawah Island
(803) 768-2121
(800) 845-2471 (SC)
(800) 654-2924
(outside SC)

Two-thousand-acre resort on ten-thousand-acre island off Charleston. Pete Dye's Ocean Course, site of the 1991 Ryder Cup, a must play with ocean views from every windswept hole.

**THE LEGENDS
GOLF CLUB
(54, PUBLIC)**
Myrtle Beach
(803) 236-9318
(800) 552-2660

Excellent facility includes The Heathlands, a British-links-style layout designed by Tom Doak. Also has a thirty-acre practice facility.

**PALMETTO
DUNES RESORT
(90, RESORT)**
Hilton Head Island
(803) 785-1138
(800) 826-1649

Two-thousand-acre oceanfront resort with five top-of-the-line layouts designed by George Fazio, Robert Trent Jones, Sr., Arthur Hills, and Robert Cupp. Two of these courses are on the Palmetto Hall site.

**SEA PINES RESORT
(54, RESORT)**
Hilton Head Island
(803) 735-3333
(800) 845-6131

Golf real estate development featuring the Pete Dye- and Jack Nicklaus-designed Harbourtown Golf Links, site of the MCI Heritage Classic.

**TIDEWATER GOLF
CLUB (18, PUBLIC)**
6,505 yards/par 72
North Myrtle Beach
(803) 249-3829
(800) 446-5363

A beautiful venue in a real estate development bordered by the Intracoastal Waterway and the Atlantic Ocean. Large bentgrass greens, well-placed bunkers, water hazards on thirteen holes, windswept.

**WILD DUNES RESORT
(36, RESORT)**
Isle of Palms
(803) 886-2164
(800) 845-8880

Tom Fazio-designed windswept links course is the golf highlight of this 1,600-acre oceanfront resort community bordered by the Atlantic Ocean and the Intracoastal Waterway.

SOUTH DAKOTA

**MEADOWBROOK
GOLF COURSE
(18, PUBLIC)**
6,520 yards/par 72
Rapid City
(605) 394-4191

Dotted with mature poplar, cottonwood, pine and other tree varieties; more than one hundred bunkers; large bentgrass greens.

TENNESSEE

LEGENDS
CLUB OF TENNESSEE
(36, PUBLIC)
Franklin
(615) 790-1300

Bob Cupp and Tom Kite
(1992) layouts, each a mix
of open linksland and tight,
well-treed fairways with
large well-protected bentgrass greens. The South
Course has a bit more
water and is tighter.

STONEHENGE
GOLF CLUB
(18, RESORT)
6,202 yards/par 72
Fairfield Glade
(615) 484-7521

Bentgrass from tee to
green, carved out of woodlands, severe elevation
changes, medium-sized,
well-bunkered undulating
greens, within real estate
development. Heatherhurst
Golf Club also on site with
twenty-seven holes.

TEXAS

BARTON CREEK
CONFERENCE RESORT
AND COUNTRY CLUB
(54, RESORT)
Austin
(512) 329-4000
(800) 336-6158

Three excellent eighteen-
hole layouts within 4,000-
acre residential
development. Designed
separately by Tom Fazio,
Ben Crenshaw and Bill
Coore, and Arnold Palmer.

FOUR SEASONS
RESORT AND CLUB
(18, RESORT)
6,451 yards/par 70
Irving
(214) 717-2530
(800) 332-3442

Jay Morrish, Byron Nel-
son, and Ben Crenshaw
venue. Rolling terrain,
medium-sized; undulating
bentgrass greens protected
by bunkers and water; wind
a factor. Private club,
Cottonwood Valley, also
on site.

HORSESHOE BAY
COUNTRY CLUB
RESORT AND
CONFERENCE
CENTER (54, RESORT)
Horseshoe Bay
(512) 598-2511
(800) 252-9363(TX),
(800) 531-5105
   (outside TX)

Three Robert Trent Jones,
Sr., layouts among the
expanses of a four-thou-
sand-acre resort on the
shoreline of Lake Lyndon
B. Johnson. Bentgrass
greens; strategically placed
bunkers; rocky rolling terrain; ravines and streams; a
variety of doglegs; stands
of oak, cedar, willow, and
persimmon.

LA CANTERA GOLF
CLUB
(18, RESORT)
6,344 yards/par 72
San Antonio
(210) 558-4653
(800) 446-5387

A Jay Morrish and Tom
Weiskopf-designed gen featuring 75 bunkers, stunning
rock outcroppings, mature
trees, a stone quarry and
dramatic elevation changes.
The 665-yard par-5 first
hole is an early indication of
thrills to come. La Cantera
is home of the Texas Open.

THE QUARRY GOLF CLUB
(18,RESORT)
6,128 yards/par 72
San Antonio
(210) 824-4500

The Quarry starts out gradually on a treeless front nine, then takes you through an 86-acre former limestone pit that drops 140 feet and offers tricky swirling winds. One of the toughest holes on this side is the 474-yard par-4 tenth, a straight long marathon called "Jack's Hammer." The back nine features jagged quarry walls, dramatic elevation changes and a scenic lake while the open front nine provides streams and lakes. the 14,500 square foot Texas Hill Country German-style-designed clubhouse provides a grand view of the entire black nine.

WATERWOOD NATIONAL COUNTRY CLUB
(18, RESORT)
6,258 yards/par 71
Huntsville
(409) 891-5211
(800) 441-5211

Situated on Lake Livingston; hilly, heavily-bunkered shotmaker's course carved from Texas pine woodlands. Medium-sized greens guarded by sand traps, mounds, trees, and water hazards.

THE WOODLANDS
(36, RESORT)
The Woodlands
(713) 367-1100
(800) 433-2624

Includes TPC Woodlands, site of PGA Tour Houston Open, and the North Course. The West and the Arnold Palmer Course, both private clubs, are on site.

UTAH

GREEN SPRING GOLF COURSE
(18, PUBLIC)
6,293 yards/par 72
Washington
(801) 673-7888

A mix of very hilly and rolling fairways, water hazards on seven holes, medium-sized undulating bentgrass greens. Shotmaker's strategic layout.

PARK MEADOWS GOLF CLUB
(18, SEMIPRIVATE)
6,666 yards/Par 72
Park City
(801) 649-2460

Nicklaus-designed Scottish links-style course in exclusive real estate development. More than one hundred sand bunkers, meandering streams, strategically placed lakes, deep rough, large undulating bentgrass greens.

VERMONT

GLENEAGLES GOLF COURSE
(18, RESORT)
6,423 yards/par 71
Manchester
(802) 362-3223

Rees Jones renovation of old Equinox Country Club, on the grounds of the Equinox Resort Hotel.

RUTLAND COUNTRY CLUB
(18, SEMIPRIVATE)
6,062 yards/par 70
Rutland
(802) 773-3254

Old-style country-club layout designed by George Low, Wayne Stiles, and John Van Kleek. Small-to-medium bentgrass greens protected by traps, back nine more tightly treed and hilly, uneven lies. Shotmaker's course.

STRATTON MOUNTAIN COUNTRY CLUB
(27, RESORT)
Stratton Mountain
(802) 297-4114
(800) 297-2200 (VT)
(800) 843-6867
   (outside VT)

Geoffrey Cornish venue. Hilly, well treed, large bentgrass greens; streams and ponds can come into play on half the holes. Site of McCall's LPGA Classic. Quality golf school on site.

SUGARBUSH
GOLF COURSE
(18, RESORT)
6,524 yards/par 72
Warren
(802) 583-2301
(800) 451-4320

Robert Trent Jones, Sr.-designed mountain course with dramatic elevation changes, tightly treed fairways, uneven lies, blind shots, tricky medium-sized undulating greens.

VIRGINIA

FORD'S COLONY
COUNTRY CLUB
(36, SEMIPRIVATE)
Williamsburg
(804) 258-4100/4130

Dan Maples layouts on rolling terrain with mature trees, ample well-trapped greens, water on approximately one-third of the holes.

THE GOLDEN HORSE-SHOE GOLF CLUB
(45, RESORT)
Williamsburg
(804) 220-7696
(800) 447-8679

Features the Gold Course, designed by Robert Trent Jones, Sr., with rolling hills, mature trees, water hazards on seven holes, small-to-medium bentgrass greens. Excellent executive course. New Rees Jones-designed Green Course set in rolling woodlands.

THE HOMESTEAD
(54, RESORT)
Hot Springs
(703) 839-5500
(800) 542-5734 (VA)
(800) 336-5771
   (outside VA)

Old-style Cascades Course or Lower Cascades (a Robert Trent Jones, Sr., design), the courses to start with at this fifteen-thousand-acre retreat dating back to the 1760s.

KINGSMILL RESORT
AND CONFERENCE
CENTER
(63, RESORT)
Williamsburg
(804) 253-1703/3906
(800) 832-5665

A 2,900-acre residential property featuring the Pete Dye-designed River Course, home of the Anheuser-Busch Golf Classic. Quality par-3 course and two additional courses designed by Arnold Palmer and Ed Seay, and Curtis Strange.

LANSDOWNE
GOLF CLUB
(18, RESORT)
6,552 yards/par 72
Leesburg
(703) 729-8400/4071
(800) 541-4801

TO GET YOU THROUGH A ROUND OF GOLF

1. "That will play."—Anonymous

2. "I know I'm getting better at golf because I'm hitting fewer spectators." —Gerald Ford

3. "Eighteen holes of match play will teach you more about your foe than nineteen years of dealing with him across a desk."—Grantland Rice

4. "Golf is a game in which you claim the privileges of age, and retain the playthings of childhood."—Samuel Johnson

5. "I don't care to belong to any club that will accept me as a member." —Groucho Marx

6. "A golfer needs a loving wife to whom he can describe the day's play through the long evenings."—P.G. Wodehouse

7. "In golf, humiliations are the essence of the game."—Alistair Cooke

8. "You drive for show and putt for dough."—Anonymous

9. "A good 1-iron shot is about as easy to come by as an understanding wife."— Dan Jenkins

10. "Never break your putter and your driver in the same round or you're dead."—Tommy Bolt

11. "Never try to play a shot you haven't practiced."—Harvey Penick

12. "Dig it out of the ground like I did."—Ben Hogan (in response to a request for instruction)

13. "I don't know why you're practicing so hard to finish second."—Babe Zaharias to an opponent

14. "I'm gonna be a Spaniard instead of a Mexkin as soon as I get some more money."—Lee Trevino just before winning his first U.S. Open in 1968

15. "He was born retired."—Jimmy Demaret on George Low, a golf hustler

16. "This will give the duffers a bit of heart."—Arnold Palmer after taking a twelve on the final round of the 1961 L.A. Open

17. "Nothing goes down slower than a golf handicap."—Bobby Nichols

18. "You're still away."—Anonymous

Robert Trent Jones, Sr.-designed layout in rolling hills of Virginia hunt country. Large undulating bentgrass greens, wind can be a factor on open front nine, back nine tighter with some dramatic elevation changes.

**THE TIDES INN
(18, RESORT)**
6,511 yards/par 72
Irvington
(804) 438-5000/5501
(800) 843-3746

The George Cobb-designed Golden Eagle Golf Course was cut out of a forest of oak, pine, and cedar. Rolling fairways, more than 120 bunkers, medium-sized undulating bentgrass greens. A well-kept secret.

**WINTERGREEN
RESORT
(36, RESORT)**
Wintergreen
(804) 325-2200
(800) 325-2200

Situated within an eleven-thousand-acre real estate development. *Stoney Creek*: A Rees Jones gem with more than one hundred bunkers, water hazards on many holes, tight back nine. *Devil's Knob*: A mountain course with magnificent views of the Blue Ridge range.

WASHINGTON

**HARBOUR POINTE
GOLF COURSE
(18, PUBLIC)**
6,487 yards/par 72
Mukilteo
(206) 355-6060

Front nine winds through twenty-eight acres of wetlands, back nine hilly and tightly treed; large bentgrass greens well guarded by traps. Course strategy and game management a must. Arthur Hills design.

**INDIAN CANYON
GOLF COURSE
(18, PUBLIC)**
6,255 yards/par 72
Spokane
(509) 747-5353

H. Chandler Egan (1935) traditional layout. Well treed; hilly; uneven lies; small tricky greens. Finesse course.

**KAYAK POINT
GOLF COURSE
(18, PUBLIC)**
6,109 yards/par 72
Stanwood
(206) 652-9676
(800) 562-3094

Penal course, dramatic elevation changes, tightly treed, bentgrass from tee to green, blind holes, 139 slope from the back tees (6,719 yards).

**MCCORMICK WOODS
(18, PUBLIC)**
6,632 yards/par 72
Port Orchard
(206) 895-0130
    /323-0130

Jack Frei design from a beautiful tree farm. Well-treed rolling fairways, bentgrass throughout, large rolling greens, grass mounds, ponds and streams, nature preserve atmosphere.

**PORT LUDLOW
GOLF AND MEETING
RETREAT
(27, RESORT)**
Port Ludlow
(206) 437-0272
(800) 732-1239

Robert Muir Graves-designed layout within a recreational real estate setting. Hilly, well treed, water hazards on half the holes, undulating large bentgrass greens, well bunkered around greens.

**SEMIAHMOO GOLF
AND COUNTRY CLUB
(18, RESORT)**
6,435 yards/par 72
Blaine
(206) 371-7005
(800) 854-2608

Rolling fairways, open, strategically placed bunkers, well-trapped large bentgrass greens, water on six holes. Arnold Palmer/Ed Seay design within eight hundred-acre real estate development.

WEST VIRGINIA

**THE GREENBRIER
(54, RESORT)**
White Sulphur Springs
(304) 536-1110
(800) 624-6070

Classic five-star mountain golf resort on 6,500 acres. Old White (1914) and Greenbrier (1924) layouts were designed by C. B. Macdonald and Seth Raynor. Lakeside (1962) is a Dick Wilson creation. Start with the Greenbrier Course.

WISCONSIN

**BLACKWOLF RUN
(36, RESORT)**
Kohler
(414) 457-4446
(800) 344-2838

Challenging Pete Dye greens near the American Club, a National Historic Landmark hotel and resort. River Course has dramatic elevation changes, large undulating, well-guarded bentgrass greens, mature trees, water hazards on twelve holes. The Meadows is more open in a Scottish links mode, with pot bunkers, very large greens, and ten water holes. An excellent but challenging venue.

**GENEVA
NATIONAL GOLF CLUB
(36, RESORT)**
Lake Geneva
(414) 245-7010

Country-club atmosphere. Features Palmer and Trevino courses with rolling hills, abundant bunkers, large greens, occasional blind shots, well-placed water hazards.

**THE GOLF COURSES
OF LAWSONIA
(36, RESORT)**
Green Lake
(414) 294-3320
(800) 558-8898

Old-style links course (1930). Open, slightly elevated greens, huge strategically placed bunkers, deep rough. A traditional golf experience. Woodlands, a Joe Lee and Rocky Roquemore design, cut out of trees, tight, hilly, with large well-protected bentgrass greens.

**SENTRYWORLD
(18, PUBLIC)**
6,286 yards/par 72
Stevens Point
(715) 345-1600

Robert Trent Jones, Jr., design. Beautifully manicured, heavily treed, with eighty-four bunkers, strategic mounds, large undulating greens; water can come into play on half the holes. Site of USGA Women's Public Links in 1986.

**UNIVERSITY RIDGE
GOLF COURSE
(18, PUBLIC)**
6,402 yards/par 72
Verona, (608) 845-8704
(800) 897-4343

Open, linkslike on front
nine, wind a factor. Back
nine tightly treed. Rolling
hills, varied subtle greens,
well bunkered. Robert
Trent Jones, Jr., layout.

WYOMING

**OLIVE GLEN GOLF
AND COUNTRY CLUB
(18, PUBLIC)**
6,515 yards/par 72
Cody
(307) 587-5551

Rolling prairie layout, large
well-guarded bentgrass
greens, water hazards on
half the holes.

**TETON PINES
COUNTRY CLUB AND
RESORT
(18, RESORT)**
6,878 yards/par 72
Jackson
(307) 733-1733
(800) 238-2223

Arnold Palmer/Ed Seay
layout with more than
forty-two acres of water.
Rolling ranch land, large
undulating bentgrass
greens protected by large
bunkers and water hazards.

Canada

**ALGONQUIN
(36, RESORT)**
St. Andrews, New
Brunswick
(506) 529-8823
(800) 268-9411

Two Donald Ross courses,
The Seaside (completed in
1900) and the Woodlands
(1921) that sit on Pas-
samaquoddy Bay two hours
northeast of Bangor,
Maine. A feast of
windswept traditional golf.

**BANFF SPRINGS
(27, RESORT)**
Banff, Alberta
(403) 762-2211
(800) 828-7447
    (from U.S.)
(800) 268-9143 (Canada)

Stanley Thompson nines
with additional nine by Bill
Robinson. Beautifully situated in Canadian Rockies
ski country near Lake
Louise.

**CARLING LAKE
(18, SEMIPRIVATE)**
6,645 yards/par 72
Pine Hill, Quebec
(514) 533-9211

A rolling, well-treed
Howard Watson (1961)
beauty situated in the Lau-
rentians, one hour north-
west of Montreal. There is
a hotel on the premises.

**BRUDENELL RIVER
(18, RESORT)**
6517 yards/par 72
Montague, Prince Edward
    Island
(902) 652-2342

A highly regarded C. E.
Robinson gem with six par-
5s, -4s, and -3s located
thirty-five miles from
Charlottetown.

**JASPER PARK
GOLF COURSE
(18, RESORT)**
6323 yards/par 71
Jasper, Alberta
(403) 852-3301
(800) 268-9143

Stanley Thompson moun-
tain course built in the
1920s with dramatic views
and elevation changes
within the one-thousand-
acre Jasper Park resort
property in the Canadian
Rockies.

**GALLAGHERS CANYON
(18, SEMIPRIVATE)**
6,494 yards/par 72
Kelowna, British Columbia
(604) 861-4240

William G. Robinson lay-
out opened in 1980 in the
hills overlooking Lake
Okanagan. This well-treed
beauty plays 6,975 yards
from the back tees.

**GLEN ABBEY GOLF
CLUB
(18, PUBLIC)**
6,618 yards/par 72
Oakville, Ontario
(416) 844-1800

Jack Nicklaus–designed site
of the Canadian Open and
home of the Royal Cana-
dian Golf Association.
Plays 7,102 yards from the
tips and is beautifully
planted with oak, maple,
spruce, and other tree varieties.

**HIGHLAND LINKS
(18, RESORT)**
6,598 yards/par 72
Cape Breton,
   Nova Scotia
(902) 285-2880

Stanley Thompson-
designed layout (1941) near
the Keltic Lodge within
Cape Breton Highlands
National Park five hours
northeast of Halifax. Small
undulating greens, unfor-
giving rough, variable
winds. No motorized carts
allowed.

**KANANASKIS COUNTRY
GOLF COURSE
(36, RESORT)**
Kananaskis Village, Alberta
(403) 591-7711
(800) 528-0444

Two courses, Mt. Kidd and
Mt. Lorrette, designed by
Robert Trent Jones in the
1980s and characterized by
large greens, strategically
placed large bunkers, water
from the Kananaskis River,
variable winds, elevation
changes, and beautiful
views of the Canadian
Rockies.

**LIONHEAD GOLF
AND COUNTRY CLUB
(27, PUBLIC)**
Brampton, Ontario
(416) 455-4900

Three Ted Baker-designed
nines that can play 7,200
yards at this $30-million
facility set on 422 acres of
meadows, wetlands, and
treed hills near Toronto.

**MILL RIVER
(18, PUBLIC)**
6,467 yards/par 72
O'Leary, Prince Edward
   Island
(902) 859-3555

A C. E. Robinson (1971)
tightly treed layout that
features large, undulating
greens and is set on three
hundred acres in Mill River
Provincial Park in western
Prince Edward Island.

**ROYAL COLWOOD
GOLF CLUB
(18, SEMIPRIVATE)**
6,543 yards/ par 70
Victoria, British
   Columbia
(604) 478-9591

A parklike gem built on
240 acres of farmland that
is now bounded by a resi-
dential communuity.
Designed by A. V. Macan
and opened in 1913.

TWIN RIVERS
GOLF COURSE
(18, PUBLIC)
6,546 yards/par 71
Port Blanford,
   Newfoundland
(709) 543-2525

Designed by C. E. Robinson (nine holes) and Doug Currick and completed in 1991, this scenic layout is situated near Terra Nova National Park and punctuated by rocks, trees, rivers, and ocean views.

WHISTLER (36. RESORT)
Whistler Village, British
   Columbia
(604) 932-3280
(800) 828-7447 (U.S.)
(800) 268-9420)

An Arnold Palmer-designed layout (1983) and a Robert Trent Jones, Jr. course (1992) at the Chateau Whistler Resort, part of the Canadian Pacific-operated chain that includes Algonquin, Banff Springs, Kananaskis, and others.

WILLOWS GOLF
AND COUNTRY CLUB
(36, SEMIPRIVATE)
Saskatoon, Saskatchewan
(306) 956-1000

These Bill Newis-designed nines (1991), Bridges, Island, Lakes and Xena can be played in any combination. Includes 33,000-square-foot clubhouse and is part of a planned community.

Bahamas, Bermuda, The Caribbean

BAHAMAS PRINCESS
(36, RESORT)
Freeport, Grand Bahama
   Island
(809) 352-9661
(800) 223-1818

A 6,679-yard Dick Wilson layout, Emerald (1964), and a 6,750-yard Joe Lee course, Ruby (1966), at the Bahamas Princess Resort and Casino.

CASTLE HARBOR
GOLF CLUB
(18, RESORT)
6,440 yards/par 71
Tuckers Town, Bermuda
(809) 293-8161
(800) 228-9290

A Charles Banks (1932) layout at Marriott's Castle Harbor Resort. Marriott invested more than $60 million in the 1980s to restore this property.

CARAMBOLA
BEACH GOLF CLUB
(18, PUBLIC)
6,843 yards/par 72
Kings Hill, St. Croix, U.S.
   Virgin Islands
(809) 778-5638

A Robert Trent Jones (1966) course in a scenic valley inland from Davis Bay and fifteen minutes from the airport.

CASA DE CAMPO
RESORT
(54, RESORT)
La Romana, Dominican
   Republic
(809) 523-3333
(800) 877-3643

Casa de Campo features Pete Dye's 6,888-yard par-72 classic, one of the best golf courses in the world. The seven-thousand-acre resort is beautifully situated on the ocean 1 1/2 hours from Santo Domingo airport.

THE FOUR SEASONS NEVIS (18, RESORT)
6766 yards/par 71
Nevis, West Indies

A scenic Robert Trent Jones, Jr., layout (1991) that wends its way down the side of a mountain to the sea. On the property of the 196-room beach-front Nevis Resort.

HALF MOON GOLF CLUB (18, RESORT)
6,582 yards/par 72
Montego Bay
   Jamaica, West Indies
(809) 953-2211
(800) 237-3237

A Robert Trent Jones design (1961) located at Half Moon Golf, Tennis, and Beach Club.

HYATT DORADO BEACH (72, RESORT)
Dorado Beach,
   Puerto Rico
(809) 799-8961
(800) 233-1234

Four Robert Trent Jones courses, including East and West (1958) at the Hyatt Dorado Beach and North and South (1971) at the Hyatt Regency Cerromar Beach, all on a one-thousand-acre property one hour from San Juan airport.

There are many travel agencies, hotel chains, associations, and tourist boards that offer golf packages and tours of various kinds. One of the strongest regional golf tourist organizations in the United States is Myrtle Beach's Myrtle Beach Golf Holiday, which promotes golf, packages, accomodations, restaurants, and various activities in the area. Quality golf tour promoters such as Golf International, Perry Golf, Intergolf, Fore International, In the English Manner, Wide World of Golf, and others offer many golf travel options, including packages to major events such as the British Open, the Ryder Cup, and the Masters. Hotel chains such as Marriott have several golf destinations, and associations such as the PGA, the Donald Ross Society, the Collectors Society, and others (see the Associations section in this book) promote tours. National tourist organizations such as the British Tourist Board and state organizations often have comprehensive lists and catalogs of golf destinations in their regions.

As you know, golfers can be very particular in their tastes, especially when it comes to choosing a place to play golf. Some golfers are wed to their local club and seldom stray from home. Others plan elaborate road trips that might involve a lifelong odyssey to play the top golf courses all over the

9

golf travel

world. Many golf travel specialists have conjured up innovative ways to please the discriminating golfer. In the British Manner combines luxury accomodations in British castles, manors, or apartments with fine cuisine and vintage golf at St. Andrews and other venues. Golf Connections of California will set you up at a weekend "Golf in the Kingdom" school with Michael Murphy. Shore Links Golf Charter will convey you along the eastern seaboard in a luxury yacht and deposit your party at Kiawah Island, Dataw Island, St. Simons Island, and other golf retreats. If you join the Donald Ross Society, you will be invited to annual events on classic Donald Ross courses such as Pinehurst No. 2 and the Panorama course at The Balsams in New Hampshire. Subscribers to the *Golf Travel* newsletter not only get regular assessments of international golf destinations, they also are offered periodic tour packages.

For those of you who favor industrial quantities of golf at low prices, off-season tours to United States golf centers such as Pinehurst, Florida, Arizona, or Myrtle Beach might be your preference. Or you can make a pilgrimage to St. Andrews and more obscure but fascinating venues in Wales or Ireland. On the United States golf travel circuit, organizations such as the American Cancer Society and the American Lung Association offer discount cards to numerous golf courses. Subscriber organizations like Golf Card International, Golf Access, and Hale Irwin's Golfer's Passport provide many discount services.

Below is a sample list of recommended travel services for your golf vacation.

GOLF TRAVEL SERVICES

Adventures in Golf
29 Valencia Drive
Nashua, NH 03062
(603) 882-8367

Ireland

Aer Lingus
122 East 42nd Street
New York, NY 10168
(212) 557-1090
(800) 223-6537

Great Britain, Ireland

Arizona Golf International
6615 N. Scotsdale Road
Scottsdale, AZ 85250
(602) 443-1344
(800) 999-6904

Arizona

The Atlantic Golf Company
237 Post Road West
Westport, CT 06880
(203) 454-0090
(800) 992-7700

Great Britain, Ireland

Atlantic Group Tours
520 Oriole Drive S.E.
Marietta, GA 30067
(404) 977-3072

Ireland

Best Golf Tours
Box 65
332 Forrest Avenue
Laguna Beach, CA 92652
(714) 752-8881
(800) 227-0212
(800) 458-6888

Ireland, Mexico, Scotland,
France, Hawaii, Arizona,
and California; also major
events such as the Masters
and the Ryder Cup

**Brian Moore
International Tours**
116 Main Street
Medway, MA 02053
(508) 533-6683
(800) 982-2299

Canada, Ireland,
Scotland

British Tourist Authority
551 Fifth Avenue
New York, New York
    10176-0799
(212) 986-2200

British Isles golf
packages and tour
information

Celtic Golf Tours
1062 Pennsylvania Avenue
Cape May, NJ 08204
(609) 884-8090
(800) 535-6148

Ireland, Scotland; also
major events
including the British Open

**Championship Golf
International**
11665 Duenda Road
San Diego, CA 92127
(619) 487-1523
(800) 222-0711

Canada, Ireland,
Scotland, Spain

Destination Ireland
250 West 57th Street
Suite 2511
New York, NY 10117
(212) 977-9629
(800) 832-1848

Great Britain, Ireland

Fore International
23200 Chagrin
    Boulevard
Suite 150
Beachwood, OH 44122
(216) 591-0105
(800) 798-FORE

U.S., Caribbean, Mexico,
England, Ireland, Scotland,
Australia, Spain, Portugal,
South Africa; also the Mas-
ters and other packages.

Genesis Sports Tours
427 Madison Avenue
New York, NY 10017
(212) 759-0480
(800) 888-8167

Ireland, Scotland

Golf Connections
13428 Maxella Avenue,
Suite 278
Marina Del Rey, CA 90292
(800) 354-4653
Fax: (310) 578-5170

"Golf in the Kingdom"
weekends with Michael
Murphy, golf outings, char-
itable events,
tournaments, meetings and
seminars

Golf Getaways Travel
30423 Canwood Street
Suite 222
Agoura Hills, CA 91301
(818) 991-7015
(800) 423-3657

Australia, France,
Ireland, Scotland

Golf Intercontinental
19 West 34th Street
Suite 302
New York, NY 10001
(212) 239-3880
(800) 223-6114

Ireland, Scotland

Golf International
275 Madison Avenue
Suite 1819
New York, NY 10016
(212) 986-9176
(800) 833-1389

Ireland, Scotland, Wales,
England, Portugal, Spain,
France

Golf Safaris
14429 Ventura
Boulevard
Suite 106
Sherman Oaks, CA 91423
(818) 556-6140

Ireland

Golf Tours Unlimited
Box 478
Bonita, CA 92002
(619) 475-6995

Scotland

Golfing Holidays
231 East Milbrae Avenue
Suite 109
Milbrae, CA 94030
(415) 697-0230

Ireland, Scotland,
England, Wales,
France, and others

Golfpac
Box 940490
901 North Lake Destiny
　Drive
Suite 192
Maitland, FL 32794
(407) 660-8277
(800) 327-0878

Ireland, Scotland,
Arizona, Florida,
Myrtle Beach

**Grasshopper
Golf Tours**
403 Hill Avenue
Glen Elyn, IL 60137
(708) 858-1660
(800) 654-8712

England, Ireland,
Scotland

Henry Hudson Tours
Box 155
Maiden-on-Hudson, NY
　12453
(914) 246-8453

Ireland

The Hidden Ireland
Box 40034
Mobile, AL 36640
(205) 433-5465
(800) 868-4750

Ireland

**Ideal Golf International
Golf Club**
P.O. Box 772
Orangeburg, SC 29116
(800) 315-9992

Scotland; Pinehurst, North
Carolina; and others

**In The
English Manner**
515 South Figueroa, Suite
1000
Los Angeles, CA
　90071-3327
(213) 629-1811
(800) 422-0799

High-end castle, manor,
apartment, and other visits
in London and the coun-
tryside of England, Ireland,
and Scotland; also golf,
sporting holidays, and
more

**Irish Links Tours &
Travel, Inc.**
2701 Summer Street
Suite 200
Stamford, CT 06905
(203) 363-2088
(800) 824-6538

Ireland

Sterling Travel
455 Paces Ferry Road
Suite 302
Atlanta, GA 30305
(404) 261-2326
(800) 447-2799

Australia, New Zealand,
England, Ireland,
Scotland, Wales, France,
Africa, Canada, and
others

ITC Golf Tours
4234 Atlantic Avenue Suite
#205
Long Beach, CA 90807
(310) 595-6905
(800) 257-4981

Australia, New Zealand,
England, Ireland, Scotland,
France, Canada, Portugal,
Spain, Kenya, South Africa,
Morrocco, and the Ivory
Coast

**French Government
Tourist Office**
610 Fifth Avenue
New York, NY
    10020-2452
(212) 757-1125

France, Martinique

Grand Slam Tours
222 Milwaukee Street
Suite 407
Denver, CO 80206
(303) 321-1760
(800) 289-3333

Australia and New Zealand

**Great Golf Resorts
of the World**
111 Presidential
    Boulevard
Suite 222
Bala Cynwyd, PA
    19004-9643
(800) 442-4479

Golf packages at The Gle-
neagles Hotel, Scotland;
The Cloister, Georgia;
The Lodge at Pebble
Beach, California; Mauna
Kea Beach Hotel, Hawaii;
Four Seasons Resort,
Nevis; and others

Hyatt Vacations
P.O. Box 98784
Chicago, IL 60693-8784
(800) 4GOLFERS

Golf Packages at Hyatt
Grand Champions Resort,
Palm Springs, California;
Hyatt Regency Cerromar
Beach Resort and Casino,
Puerto Rico; and several
others

Intergolf
P.O. Box 500608
Atlanta, GA 31150-0608
(800) 468-0051

Canada, Morocco, South
Africa, France, Portugal,
Spain, Austria, Hungary,
Scandanavia, England,
Wales, Ireland, Scotland,
Australia, New
Zealand;major events such
as the British Open; and
cruises to the Caribbean,
Mexico, and the South
Pacific

**John Jacobs Golf &
Travel**
7825 East Redfield Road
Scottsdale, AZ
    85260-6977
(602) 483-2016
(800) 822-1255

Arizona, Florida, Califor-
nia, Hawaii, Australia, New
Zealand, Scotland, Ireland,
Spain, and Malaysia; also
major events such as the
Masters and the British
Open

**Leisure Destinations
Marketing**
Box 220
Palm City, FL 34990
(407) 220-0410

Scotland

Lynott Tours
350 Fifth Avenue
Suite 2619
New York, NY 10118
(212) 760-0101
(800) 221-2474

England, Ireland, Scotland, Wales, Australia, New Zealand, Fiji, and New Guinea

Marriott Corporation
Marriott Drive
Washington, DC 20058
(301) 380-2580
(800) 228-9290

Twenty Marriott golf resorts, including Puerto Vallarta, Mexico; Marriott at Sawgrass Resort, Ponte Vedra, Florida; and Marriott's Seaview Resort, Absecon, New Jersey

Myrtle Beach Golf Holiday
609 Seaboard Street
Box 1323
Myrtle Beach, SC 29578-1323
(800) 845-4653

Packages to over seventy golf courses in the Myrtle Beach area

Northwest Worldvacations
5130 Highway 101
Minnetonka, MN 55345
(612) 470-1111
(800) 727-1111

Scotland

Owenoak International
88 Main Street
New Canaan, CT 06840
(203) 972-3777
(800) 426-4498

Ireland, Wales, and Scotland

Perry Golf
8302 Dunwoody Place
Suite 305
Atlanta, GA 30350
(404) 641-9696
(800) 344-5257

England, Ireland, Scotland, Portugal, Spain, South Africa, Australia, and New Zealand; also the British Open and other major events

PGA Travel
3680 North Peachtree Road
Atlanta, GA 30341
(800) 283-4653

Australia, Ireland, Scotland, Spain, and Canada. Also several U.S. resorts, inluding PGA National & Spa, Florida; The Broadmoor, Colorado; and Kiawah Island, South Carolina

Phelan Golf
Box 1222
Darien, CT 06820
(203) 655-8084
(800) 274-7888

England, Ireland, and Scotland

Scottish Golf Holidays
9403 Kenwood Road
Suite A 205
Cincinnati, OH 45242
(513) 984-0414
(800) 284-8884

England, Ireland, and Scotland; major tournaments; and leading golf resorts

Shore Links Golf Charter
49 Bowen's Wharf
Newport, RI 02840
(800) 732-6465
Fax: (401) 849-3325

Small-group golf/yacht tours at scenic coastal resorts from Maine to Florida

Showcase Ireland
586 Roma Court
Naples, FL 33963
(813) 591-3447
(800) 654-6527

Customized trips to
Ireland

Travel Concepts
373 Commonwealth
   Avenue
Suite 601
Boston, MA 02115
(617) 266-8450

Groups of fifteen or more,
Scotland and the British
Open

**TravelTix
International**
400 Madison Avenue
Suite 411
New York, NY 10017
(212) 688-3700

England, Ireland, Scotland,
Wales, Portugal, Spain,
France, Morrocco, Italy,
Australia, New Zealand,
Canada, the Caribbean,
domestic U.S., and others

**VALLEY ISLE
GOLF TOURS**
P.O. Box 556
Kihea, Hawaii 96753
(800) 558-9117

Hawaiian Islands, espe-
cially Maui

Value Holidays
10224 North Port
   Washington Road
Mequon, WI 53092
(414) 241-6373
(800) 558-6850

Ireland, Scotland

Value Golf Vacations
260 Fifth Avenue
New York, New York
   10001
(212) 986-0393
(800) 786-7634

Ireland and Scotland and
major events such as the
British Open

Vignette Holidays
270 North Canon Drive
Suite 1053
Beverly Hills, CA 90210
(213) 479-3160,
(800) 776-7660

Custom-designed tours for
Britain and Europe

Wide World of Golf
Box 5217
Carmel, CA 93921
(800) 214-4653
(408) 624-6667

Ireland, Scotland, Portugal,
Spain, Australia, New
Zealand, South Africa,
Mexico, Hawaii, and Peb-
ble Beach; major events
such as the Ryder Cup, and
cruises to the Caribbean
and elsewhere

**World Golf
Hospitality, Inc.**
7000 Peachtree
Dunwoody Road
Lake Ridge Office Park
Bldg. 4, Suite 250
Atlanta, GA 30328
(404) 399-0505,
Fax: (404) 399-0620

Australia, New Zealand,
England, Ireland, Scotland,
Wales, Europe, Africa,
Canada, and the United
States

Most golf resorts have seasonal discount rates and golf packages to ease the financial pain of playing golf. Most daily-fee courses have twilight rates, residential, junior, senior citizen, seasonal, and multiple play discounts of various kinds. There are also organized national discount programs, including Golf Card International's travel-card club that provides a network of golf discounts at participating courses in the United States, Canada, and other locations. Golf Card International publishes a quarterly magazine, *Golf Traveler*, that provides announcements of new affiliate clubs, special golf package offers, golf-school information, "Grasshopper Club" schedules where members convene for informal matches, and other useful information. Contact: Golf Card International, 1637 Metropolitan Boulevard, Suite C, Talahassee, FL 32308, (800) 522-9232.

The American Cancer Society sponsors a variety of discount plans including the Florida Discount Card, which offers seasonal and year-round discount plans on over three hundred of Florida's courses. Contact: The American Cancer Society, 3710 W. Jefton Avenue, Tampa, FL 333629-5122, (800) ACS-2345. The American Lung Association also offers golf privilege-card programs. Over four hundred golf courses in the United States and British Columbia participate in this program. Contact: American Lung Association, Golf Privilege Card, 1510 San Andrews Street, Santa Barbara, CA 93101 (800) LUNG-USA. Hotel discount plans are offered at over 2,100 properties.

If you are having difficulty finding a discount plan in your region, there are additional programs. Hale Irwin's Golfer's Passport, P.O. Box 220067, St. Louis, MO 63122, (800) 334-3140, includes over 1,500 participating courses in the United States, Mexico, Canada, Australia, and the Caribbean. Golf Access has more than 1,700 U.S. and Caribbean courses in its network and offers discounts on resorts, hotels, condominiums, motels, car rentals, airfare, cruises, and motor-home rentals. Contact: Access Development Corporation, P.O. Box 27563, Salt Lake City, UT 84127-0563, (801) 262-2233, (800) 359-4653.

10

golf collectibles

Golf collecting no doubt began several hundred years ago in the British Isles when clubs and balls were handed down from generation to generation. In 1743 *The Goff: An Heroi Comical Poem in Three Cantos*, the first book completely dedicated to golf, mentioned a golf collection, and in the 1860s one of the earliest-known golf museums opened in the Union Club House in St. Andrews, Scotland. The Union Club later merged with the Royal and Ancient Club of St. Andrews in 1877 and it is believed that many items in the current collection at the R & A came from the Union Club.

Serious private collections of clubs, balls, books, art, and other golf collectibles began to evolve in the late nineteenth century. The first comprehensive study of golf memorabilia, according to *The Encyclopedia of Golf Collectibles*, written by John M. and Morton W. Olman, leading collectibles authorities from Ohio, was *Golfing Curios and the Like*, compiled by Harry B. Wood in 1910. Wood later donated his collection to the North Manchester (England) Golf Club, where it currently resides. Small museums at golf clubs and private collections gradually expanded as equipment evolved, more golf courses were developed, the game became more popular, and more was published about the subject. Prior to 1900 there were few golf courses in the United States, but by 1930 there were more than 5,700 golf courses and approximately 9,000 worldwide. Golf had evolved from the idle pastime of shepherds to a leisure sport played under the governance of rules committees, most notable the Royal and Ancient and the United States Golf Association.

The Great Depression and World War II slowed up the growth, but after World War II golf became more popular and accessible, as did collecting. The United States Golf Association began to acquire memorabilia and opened a museum and library at Golf House in 1950. In 1970, The Golf Collector's Society was formed in the United States. More recently, the large auction houses such as Christie's and Sotheby's have been holding spirited golf-memorabilia auctions. Today early feathery golf balls can fetch several thousand dollars, as can rare golf clubs.

The scope of golf collectibles has broadened from golf equipment and books to golf tees, scorecards, stamps, pencils, and tee-shirts. Golf museums are being expanded, and new exhibits are being opened at clubs around the world. The United States Golf Association in Far Hills, New Jersey; the Ralph W. Miller Museum and Library in City of Industry, California; and established clubs such as Winged Foot, the Royal and Ancient Golf Club, the James River Country Club, and the Foxburg Country Club are rich sources for viewing golf collectibles.

Below is a brief bibliography of book sources on collection. Also, refer to the Book and Museums and Collections sections of this book for additional resources.

Golf Collectibles and Collecting

BOOK SOURCES

Clement, Joe. *Classic Golf Clubs: A Pictorial Guide.* Jackson, MS: Classic Golf Clubs, 1980.

Donovan, Dick, and Joe Murdoch. *The Game of Golf and the Printed Word, 1566–1985: A Bibliography of Golf Literature in the English Language.* Endicott, NY: Castalio Press, 1988.

Fabian-Baddiel, Sarah. *Miller's Golf Memorabilia.* London, England: Reed International, 1994.

Geogiady, Peter. *Compendium of British Clubmakers.* North Carolina: Airlie Hall Press, 1994.

Henderson, Ian T., and David I. Stirk. *Golf in the Making: Revised.* London: Sean Arnold, 1990.

Hopkinson, Cecil, and Joseph S.F. Murdoch. *Collecting Golf Books 1743–1938.* Droitwich, England: Grant Books, 1980.

Johnston, Alistair J. and Murdoch, Joseph S.F. *C. B. Clapcott and His Golf Library*. Droitwich, England: Grant Books, 1988.

Kennedy, Patrick. *Golf Club Trademarks— American: 1898-1930*. South Burlington, VT: Thistle Books, 1984.

Kelly, Leo M., Jr. *Antique Golf Ball and Reference Price Guide*. Richton Park, IL: Old Chicago Golf Shop, 1993.

Kuntz, Bob, and Mark Wilson. *Antique Golf Clubs: Their Restoration and Preservation*. Endicott, New York: Castalio Press, 1990.

Martin, John Stuart. *The Curious History of the Golf Ball: Mankind's Most Fascinating Sphere*. New York: Horizon Press, 1968.

Mathew Sidney L. *The History of Bobby Jones' Clubs*. Limited edition, 1993.

Murdoch, Joseph S.F. *The Library of Golf, 1743-1966*. Detroit: Gale Research, 1968, revised edition 1978

Olman, John M., and Morton W. Olman. *Olman's Guide to Golf Collectibles: A Collector's Identification and Value Guide*. Florence: Books Americana, 1985.

—Olman's Guide to Golf Antiques and Other Treasures of the Game. Cincinnati: Market Street Press, 1992.

Robb, Beverly. *Collectible Golfing Novelties*. Pennsylvania: Schiffer Publishing, 1992.

Schwartz, Gary H. *The Art of Golf: 1754-1940: Timeless, Enchanting Illustrations and Narrative of Golf's Formative Years*. Tiburon, CA: Wood River Publishing, 1990.

Seagle, Janet. *The Club Makers*. Far Hills, New Jersey: United States Golf Association, 1989.

Smith, Robert A. *Golf Club U.S. Patent Index* 1894-1940.

Sprung, Shirley and Jerry. *Decorative Golf Collectibles*. Coral Springs, Florida: H.F.G. Witherby Ltd., 1991, 1992.

Stirk, David. *Golf: The Great Clubmakers*. Longdon: H.S.G. Witherby, 1992.

Watt, Alick A. *Collecting Old Golfing Clubs*. Alton, England: Published by the Author, 1985.

Wilson, Mark. *The Golf Identification and Price Guide III: 1950 to 1993*. Newark, Ohio: Ralph Maltbie, 1993.

Wood, Harry B. *Golfing Curios and the Like*. 1910. Reprint edition, Manchester: Pride Publishers, 1980.

Auction Houses and Collectibles Dealers

This short list of auction houses and dealers in golf memorabilia provides a network for discovering more about golf collectibles, as does the Golf Collectors Society.

Sarah Baddiel
The Golf Gallery
42 Hertford Street
Cambridge CB43AG
O 223 357 958

Equipment, books, periodicals, and other memorabilia

David Berkowitz
1252 West Illinois Avenue
Palatine, IL 60067
(708) 934-4108

Art, balls, ceramics, silver, and other collectibles

Burchfield's
Box 1205
One Market Square
Village of Pinehurst
    NC 28374
(910) 295-6842,
(800) 358-4006

Prints, clubs, memorabilia displays, and other items

Christie's
502 Park Avenue
New York, NY 10022
(212) 606-0460
(212) 546-1000

Periodic auctions, including clubs, book, balls, prints, and other collectibles

Richard E. Donovan Enterprises
Publishers and
    Booksellers
Box 7070
305 Massachusetts Avenue
Endicott, NY 13760
(607) 785-5874

Specialists in new and antique golf publications

Colonel John C. Furness
Crossway House
Trotherwald, Dumfries
DG1 3PT, Scotland

Clubs, balls, and other collectibles

The Golf Collectors Society
P.O. Box 20546
Dayton, OH 45420
(513) 256-2474

Publishes a directory of members and their collecting interests and organizes shows where collectibles are exhibited and sold

Bob Grant
The Coach House
New Road
Curnawall Green
Worcestershire WR9 OPQ
England
012 9985 588

Clubs, balls, and other collectibles

Leo Kelly
4977 Arquilla Drive
Richton Park, IL 60471
(708) 747-1045

Art, books, balls, clubs, ephemera, and more

**George
Lewis/Golfiana**
P.O. Box 291
Mamaroneck, NY 10543
(914) 698-4579

Art, books, periodicals,
ephemera, and other
collectibles

Kevin McGrath
47 Leonard Road
Melrose, MA 02176
(617) 662-6588

Art, clubs, books, prints,
ephemera, and more

The Old Golf Shop
325 West Fifth Street
Cincinnati, OH 45202
(513) 241-7797

Art, books, periodicals,
memorabilia, ephemera,
and other collectibles

**Old Troon
Sporting Antiques**
46 Ayr Street
Troon, Ayrshire,
Scotland
KA 106EB
0292 311822
Fax: 0292 313111

Art, clubs, balls, and other
collectibles

THE GOLF COLLECTORS SOCIETY

The Golf Collectors Society was founded by J. Robert Kuntz, co-author of *Antique Golf Clubs: Their Restoration and Preservation* with Mark Wilson, and Joseph S.F. Murdoch, noted golf-book collector and author of the landmark *The Murdoch Golf Library* documenting his collecting and collection. The Society started with a total of twenty-seven members and has expanded to a larger but still colleagial body of over 2500 collectors from fourteen countries.

The Golf Collector's Society has local chapters, a membership directory, a newsletter, and a three-day annual meeting held each fall, featuring auctions, seminars, a "Hickory Hacker Open" played with hickory shafted clubs, and other activities. When you sign up for membership in the Society, you are asked to state your membership objectives and profile your collecting interests by chosing from over forty categories. The Golf Collectors Society costs only $35 to join (U.S. residents) and slightly more for international members. The Society emphasizes education, information exchange, and shared golf fellowship. GOLF COLLECTORS SOCIETY, P.O. Box 20546, Dayton, OH 45420, (513) 256-2474.

Oliver's
Box 337
Kennebunk, ME 04043
(207) 985-3600

Periodic auctions of art, clubs, balls, and other collectibles

Phillips
406 East 79th Street
New York, NY 10021
(212) 570-4830

Periodic auctions of art, clubs, balls, and other collectibles

Richard Ulrich, Sr.
113 Walnut St., #85
Neptune, NJ 07753
(908) 988-9681

Art, books, balls, clubs, and more

Sotheby's
1334 York Avenue
New York, NY 10021
(212) 606-7000

Periodic auctions including clubs, balls, art, silver, books, and other memorabilia

Anything from golf tees to collectibles can be obtained through specialized golf catalogs such as those offered by associations (the USGA, the National Golf Foundation, and others), as well as through more general catalogs available from golf-equipment manufacturers, golf retailers, book and video distributors, tour companies, and others. As specialized cable, online, and other interactive direct-marketing services are developed, golf merchandise, collectibles, information, and other products will become more readily available.

11

golf merchandise catalogs

One of the best places to view a complete range of golf merchandise and see what the latest trends are in the golf material world is the PGA International Golf Show held annually at the end of January in Orlando, Florida. This is the meeting where many of the PGA's more than 22,000 members and apprentices from its forty-one sections in the United States gather to buy, sell, and pursue many versions of the golfer's dream. Manufacturers, club professionals, agents, buyers, publishers, distributors, media people, and other golf fellow travellers from all over the world gather at the PGA show. Approximately 2,000 booths include major players such as Wilson, Daiwa,

Callaway, Titleist, *Golf Magazine*, and Cobra, as well as lesser known entrepreneurs.

Exhibitors are classified into groups dealing with all aspects of golf, including golfing accessories: apparel for men; apparel for women; architects and designers; associations and service organizations; awards, trophies, and tees companies; bag storage racks and systems; bags, carryalls, and luggage; balls; battery charger systems; golf cars and carts; club components; club manufacturers; repair and refinishing products; clubs; computer systems and software; crests and emblems; display fixtures; gifts; gloves; grips; hats, caps, and visors; headcovers; jewelry and watches; lockers and benches; publications; purses and handbags; rainwear and windbreakers; range equipment; resorts; score cards and print products; scoring systems; shafts; shoes; teaching and training aids; tee, course, and shop signage; tour and travel services; towels; umbrellas; video systems and tapes; and, of course, miscellaneous.

The aforementioned tedious list of categories indicates how big, competitive, and perhaps overcrowded the golf business has become. There are almost one hundred headcover manufacturers and seventy-five golf glove producers alone. All of this mercantile dynamism provides the golf consumer with boundless choices. Would you like four headcovers that resemble gophers? No problem. Or perhaps you'd like a forged oversized 6-iron that will cut through bermuda grass like a weed whacker. Step right over here.

Following is a short list of the more noteworthy catalogs. Many of the associations, museums, tour operators, manufacturers, and others covered elsewhere in this book also offer mail-order and telephone purchase options. Should you wish to inquire about the PGA International Golf Show, contact: PGA of America, 100 Avenue of the Champions, Box 109601, Palm Beach Gardens, FL 33410-9601, (407) 624-8400, Fax (407) 624-8585.

Golf Catalogs

Austads
4500 East 10th Street
Box 1428
Sioux Falls, SD 57196
(800) 759-4653
Fax: (605) 339-0362

Training aids, videos, clubs, ball holders, balls, apparel, grips, shoes, umbrellas, accessories

British Links
Golf Classics
5429 Beltline
Dallas, TX 75240
(800) 348-4646
(214) 696-8403

Collectibles, bronze limited editions, ball and club display racks, prints, photos, signs, hole replicas, club reproductions, golf-course maps, bookends, golf clocks, great golf-course videos

Competitive Edge Golf
526 West 26th Street 10th Floor
New York, New York 10001
(800) 433-4465
Fax: (212) 924-3838

Clubs, bags, balls, apparel, training aids, accessories

Golf Day
375 Beacham Street
Chelsea, MA 02150
(800) 669-8600

Apparel, accessories, clubs, bags, training aids, grips, books, carts, club components

GolfSmart
Box 639
Chicago Park, CA 95712
(800) 637-3557
(916) 272-1422

BOOKS, VIDEO

Golf Fantastic
6637 North Sidney Place
Glendale, WI 53209
(800) 558-3058
(414) 351-7070
Fax: (414) 351-6907

The Duck Press
Box 1147
San Marcos, CA 92069
(800) 233-2730
(619) 471-1115
Fax: (619) 591-0990

Golf gift items including T-shirts, towels, mugs, greeting cards, and other merchandise

Edwin Watts
Golf Shop
Box 1806
Fort Walton Beach, FL 32459
(800) 342-7103 (in FL)
(800) 874-0146 (nationwide)
Fax: (904) 244-5217

Clubs, bags, balls, apparel, grips, shafts, videos, books, accessories

Field & Associates
269 Southeast 5th Avenue
Delray Beach, Fl 33483
(407) 278-0545
Fax: (407) 278-8463

Tournament gifts, awards, sponsor gifts

Herrington
3 Symmes Drive
Londonderry, NH 03050
(800) 903-2878
Fax: (603) 437-3492

Clubs, bags, apparel, training aids, collectors cabinets, books, videos, accessories, and non-golf high-end gadgets

Golf Arts & Imports
Dolores near 6th
Box 5217
Carmel, CA 93921
(408) 625-4488

Prints, books, apparel,
collectibles

Golfsmith
10206 North IH-35
Austin, TX 78753
(512) 837-4810
(800) 456-3344
Fax: (512) 837-1245

Apparel, balls, clubs,
books, greeting cards, tees,
gloves, bags, shoes, training aids, grips

The Golfworks
Ralph Maltby
Enterprises, Inc.
4820 Jacksontown Road
Box 3008
Newark, OH
43058-3008
(800) 848-8358
(614) 323-4193
   (outside U.S. and
   Canada)
Fax: (800) 800-3290
(614) 323-0311
   (outside U.S. and
   Canada)

Machines, tools, and
gauges; clubheads; compo-
nents and supplies for golf
repair shops, manufactur-
ers, custom clubmakers,
and do-it-yourselfers;
videos and books

JEF World of Golf
1225A Greenbriar
Addison, IL 60101
(708) 268-6340
Fax: (708) 268-9480

Training aids, golf
 accessories

**Las Vegas
Golf and Tennis**
5325 S. Valley View
  Boulevard
Las Vegas, NV 89118
(800) 933-7777
(702) 798-7777
Fax: (702) 798-6847

Marketcraft
Heritage Drive
Portsmouth, NH 03801
(603) 436-7983
Fax: (603) 436-3417

**Maryco Products-The
Golf People**
7215 Pebblecreek Road
W. Bloomfield, MI 48322
(800) 334-7757
(313) 851-4597

Prizes and awards, including trophies, clothing,
accessories, glassware and
other items.

Prize Possessions
203 Carnegie Row
Norwood, MA 02062
(800) 283-1166
(617) 762-8235
Fax: (617) 762-1729

Prizes and awards,
including cut glass, clocks,
silver trays, prints,
decanters, statuary, picture
frames, bookends, ice
buckets, monogrammed
playing-card sets, chairs,
club and ball holders, and
other items

**United States
Golf Association**
Golf House
Box 708
Far Hills, NJ 07931
(800) 336-4446
(908) 234-9687
Fax: (908) 234-9687

Books, videos, pamphlets,
golf collectibles, acces-
sories, apparel, and other
items, including USGA-
logoed merchandise